The
SWEET
GOSPEL

Dedication

This book is lovingly dedicated to the memory of
our Pastor Jim sweet (1918 - 2010) and his wife Joyce.

With all our love and gratitude,
Barbara Payne and Dennis Rigg.

Copyright © 2020

All rights reserved. No part of this publication can be reproduced or transmitted in any form or by any means without permission in writing from the Author.

Scripture verses are mainly quoted from the King James Version (KJV).

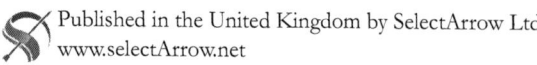
Published in the United Kingdom by SelectArrow Ltd.
www.selectArrow.net

ISBN: 9798652987541

Compiled and collated by BARBARA Payne
Email: *paynebarbara7@gmail.com*

Cover and interior design: Homer Slack
Editor: Angela Slack

Acknowledgements

A big thank you to my husband John Payne, who painstakingly encouraged me during the compilation of Jim Sweet's story. Most of all, I thank you Lord Jesus for allowing Dennis Rigg and myself to be part of Jim and Joyce's life and that you gave them to us to teach us the 'ways of the Lord'. They were our spiritual parents in every way. Jim was a great encourager and I even sensed him encouraging me as I wrote his story.

Secondly, I want to thank Homer and Angela Slack whose heart for the gospel of Christ was evident as they also encouraged me to continue writing Jim's story. You are a blessing to me and to the Body of Christ.

Testimonials

I worked for Jim Sweet at Linton Textiles, Rochdale for many years. He was a very calm and quiet man to work alongside.

He was admired because he was also a wonderful designer creating cardigans, jumpers etc. many of them which were used for Marks and Spencer's stores. One of the ladies at work knew I was into photography and asked if I would go to Radcliffe Tabernacle Church and take photos of the baptisms.

When I arrived I sat on the front row and when Jim got up to speak I was dumbfounded to see a totally different man from the one I knew at work. His passion for the gospel was very evident. Where was the quite calm man I knew? Needless to say I got more than I bargained for, for I gave my heart to the Lord. I felt on fire when I got home and even today the memory is very clear, the first chorus we sang was, "Bless the Lord Oh my soul."

Mervyn Rigg

Testimonials Continued

I was privileged to know Jim and Joyce from joining Hebron Pentecostal Church, Failinge, Rochdale. It began in 1978. Then they started a Church in Radcliffe which I used to visit. I had a very close relationship with Jim and Joyce over the years and Joyce also was involved in The Women's Aglow ministry in Heywood, now called Aglow International. Both Jim and Joyce were very influential in my life, my husband Roy's and my children.

They shared the Love of Christ in many ways. Jim always preached a message of salvation that touched your heart. His enthusiasm for people to see the glory of God in their lives was so evident. His walk with the Lord was to praise Him constantly and he always had a big smile on his face, shining with the glory of the Lord. He loved to teach the Bible and was so instrumental in many people's lives. He walked the walk denying himself for the sake of others. Jesus just shone from his heart. A wonderful display of God's love and grace. He was always willing to share with you and encourage your growth in Jesus. Great man of God. They were always loved in our hearts.

Jean Wood (President - Women's Aglow, Heywood)

Testimonials Continued

I first met Jim and Joyce Sweet as a child, in my Baptist church. During worship I used to think it was, 'who can sing the loudest competition' between Jim and the other men as they pelted out in full gusto... 'years I've spent in vanity and pride at Calvary!!!' As they would tap their mission praise books against their legs like a drum beat, never opening them to see the words. I soon learnt that the man singing the loudest was actually praising God, the King of Kings for who He was and what He had done in his life, giving praise to the Lord for His salvation.

When I came back to the Lord in my 20s, both Jim and Joyce stood with open arms, like the Father with the prodigal son, so warm full of love and pleased to see me back. This couple helped me through some tough times, spent hours praying with me and ministering into my life. They helped me deal with the hurts and pains from my childhood. Realising these I found who I was in God, what my gifting and ministry was and who God had called me to be.

They confirmed a word spoken over me as a child and now that has come to light. Where the Bible says that Jesus came to earth to seek and save the lost, I also believe that this wonderful couple had the same mission in life. They were always sharing about Jesus, the love and miracles, the blessings of God and how Jesus can change your life around. How blessed I am to have known them and been under their ministry, in fact I'm so blessed, just in Joyce's last few years she handed me her Bible and said she wanted me to have it, she needed a larger print but the Holy Spirit prompted her to give this to me. Now and then I pick up Joyce's Bible and I am still amazed at how God today ministers to me through His word and from someone else's study Bible too. I thank God now for their ministry, their time and Godly wisdom and for also being spiritual grandparents to me.

Gemma Swarbrick
Elim Pentecostal Church Kirkholt (leading in praise and worship)

Testimonials Continued

Well, what we remember about Jim and Joyce was the joy of the Lord, even when we felt sad he brought joy to us both. We remember going to his Bible study and even though we weren't really well versed in the Bible, he explained it for us to understand. Jim was a big giant but kind and gentle. (He also called his wife his 'wifee.')

We first met Jim while we were doing a mothers' and toddlers' group at Zion Baptist Church. He joined in with us and everyone loved him, young and old. He would burst into a song anywhere, anytime. The song we will never forget is, "I'll never be the same again, oh no."

It was a pleasure to have known him.
Thank you Pastor Sweet

Love John and Cath Johnston, Rochdale

Testimonials Continued

I Remember Jim Sweet, he came from Llanhilleth in Monmouthshire. He was a good preacher and the first Pastor at the Pentecostal church in Congleton. I was a youth leader there for a while in the early seventies when the Unitarian Church in Cross Street became vacant as the Pentecostals had bought it. After Jim Sweet retired Fred Howell became Pastor and then Andrew Calvert.

Robert New Alsager

Testimonials Continued

I became a Christian in 1979 after attending Radcliffe Tabernacle. The minister there was Pastor Jim Sweet and his wife Joyce. They took us under their spiritual wings and Jesus became more and more real in my life.

When I was much younger I was in the boy scouts, which was aligned to St Thomas's Church at Kirkholt in Rochdale and in the few years of involvement there was never any revelation of who Jesus was and the music was listless and very clinical (and I was in the Choir). Walking into Radcliffe Tabernacle on that wonderful day in 1979 was so different, it was just alive in the Spirit, the people oozed love and joy. The reality of Jesus was revealed through the praise and worship which was uninhibited and full of joy and the Holy Spirit.

When Pastor Sweet preached it was a continuation of the praise and worship; the passion for the gospel (good news of Christ) was self-evident and the conviction of God's word lay heavy on me. When the appeal came to commit myself to the Lord, it was instant and I sobbed my way to the foot of the cross. Jim always preached the cross of Christ and resurrection from the dead. "If I preach not Christ crucified my preaching is in vain." I remember a chorus we used to sing, "I'll never be the same again, Oh no" and that is so true. That doesn't mean to say that the past 41 years have been easy because it hasn't. Has it made me a perfect Christian? Definitely not, what I can say is my faith is still strong and Jesus is more real to me now than when the journey started.

After being baptised I felt a complete renewal in myself albeit the night prior to being baptised my wife and I had an unholy row. When we spoke with Jim and Joyce they said something to the effect that it was the devil's last attempt to drag us back and was not uncommon.

Ministering Angel

One of the Highlights of my Christian walk was when, in one of my darkest moments, I had a visitation from what I can only describe as an Angel. It was a winter's evening and I had just driven back from the office in Farnworth, Manchester and I was sitting in my usual armchair watching Barbara [my wife at the time] playing a board game on the floor with our two boys. She knew nothing of what I was going through, I must have dozed off momentarily and it could only have been a couple of minutes because I could hear them playing, as I opened my eyes there was a figure standing at the opposite side of the chimney breast. He startled me but there was no fear, he stood about seven feet tall and had blonde hair and blue eyes with a wonderful peaceful smile and without opening his mouth what I received was just peace and "everything is going to be alright". The one thing that stood out to me was his brilliant white suit which he was wearing because it wasn't being worn on him but it seemed to be part of him and was perfect. My eyes were fixed on him but were aware of Barbara and the lads playing their board game. After a short while as I glanced down and as I looked again he had gone. I felt at peace for the first time in quite a while.

When I visited Jim at his home I relayed this experience and immediately he said, " You have been visited by an Angel brother.

Hebrews 1:14 - *"Are not all angels ministering spirits sent to serve those who will inherit salvation?"*

Jim was an inspired preacher and teacher and we were honoured to sit under his ministry, the church was always full, people will always go where they are fed (spiritually). As I write this, I realise the level of his commitment to his ministry, considering he worked full time as well as in his ministry and would not accept any financial reward.

Acts 4:36 talks about Barnabas (son of encouragement). He was not so well known as an apostle but Barnabas took hold of Saul who later became 'Paul the apostle'. Many of the early Church were scared of him after the persecution and the stoning of Stephen but Barnabas united Paul with the early Church speaking up for him and giving him the credibility and so Paul went on to write much of the New Testament.

Thank God for the Christians who encourage others to do more for the sake of the Gospel. Well, Jim and Joyce Sweet were both the modern-day Barnabas and have left behind a wonderful legacy.

One day we will meet again and what a glorious day that will be.

Dennis Rigg, retired Pastor Rochdale.

Foreword

I will never forget the night I surrendered my life to Jesus, He instantly became real to me even though I did not understand the full implication of what I had done or why I felt compelled to do it. It was in Radcliffe Tabernacle Lancashire. As a child I had been in the local choir in my hometown of Chesterton, Newcastle-Under-Lyme in the Church of England but I had never heard the gospel of Jesus Christ like this before. It was such a warm, happy and vibrant church and everyone seemed so full of joy. They sang about Jesus like they knew Him and the preacher, Jim Sweet, even cried when he talked about Jesus on the cross. This was all new to me. Even though I knew nothing of the Bible I just knew everything he was saying about Jesus was true…there was an 'inner witness' that I later realised was the Holy Spirit witnessing to my spirit. I was enthralled but it was when Jim finally said, 'Jesus put two arms up for you, can't you put one up for Him?' Well my arm shot in the air as if I had been pierced through. I became 'born again' the very same second. Well that was my first encounter with Jesus…fantastic, and I just knew that I knew that something special had happened to me. I also had an immediate assurance that I was heaven bound. All my past seemed to rush in front of me and I started to cry as I realised God's love had reached out to even me. I was thirty two years old. This is the greatest mysterious miracle that happens to all who will believe in the Lord Jesus Christ and His atoning work upon the cross.

*(from **'Reach for Your Miracle'** by Barbara Ann Payne)*

That was over 40 years ago and the reason for putting this book together is first to honour God and secondly to honour Jim Sweet and his servant heart for the passion of the Gospel of Jesus Christ that never changed in all the years that I had known him. A true man of God.

After being born again we received a visit from Jehovah's Witnesses and they wanted to talk about 'the end of the world'. As I did not know anything about it I rang Jim and asked if he could teach me the book of Revelation. He laughed and asked me why and then invited us to his home. I thought it would take about 6 weeks but 3 and half years later we were still studying the amazing book and we developed a love for God's Word that led us into ministering and serving the Lord all these years. From evangelism, worship, intercession and prayer leading men and women's groups and travelling to preach the gospel and God's word, and eventually leading and pastoring a church in Rochdale plus so much more. The grounding that Jim and Joyce gave us was rock solid built on God's Word alone and I am so grateful to God for providing such a man as Jim Sweet to teach, admonish and encourage us in the work of the Lord. The Bible study group went on for 20 years and they never invited anyone, God just sent people who were hungry for the Word of God.

I visited Jim and Joyce when they were unfortunately in a care home together and the last thing we did together was sing the song he taught us just after I got saved. He hardly recognised me but as soon as we began to sing... there was Jim. We sang, "Sheltered in the Arms of God," but his favourite song was:

I'll never be the same again O no;
I'll never be the same again O no;
Since I met the Lord I am not the same;
I'll never be the same again.

He would then raise a Hallelujah leg.

They both died shortly afterwards within a space of 6 weeks from each other. A wonderful lasting memory of a wonderful spiritual father and mother in Christ.

It is with a grateful heart that I wanted to put together just a few of his sermons surrounded by just a little of what he accomplished in the 59 years he served God. I have only compiled his own writings so really this is his book and his account of some of his life's work for Jesus.

It has been a privilege to type it up through laughter and of course tears but I know he is now raising a Hallelujah leg in glory. So until we meet again, thank you Jim and of course Joyce.

Barbara Ann Payne

Contents

Section 1 - Jim Sweet's Testimony

War and Narrow Escapes From Death 1

Making A New Start 9

The Call to Build a Church 15

The Call to the FGBMI 21

Section 2 - Jim Sweet's Sermons

Four Stages of Life 29

He Lingered 35

Why Did He Love us so? - Just Because! 41

Corinthians 1:17 49

Lifted Up 53

Humility 59

Kingdom 63

Revival 67

Believed 73

Glorified in His Saints 79

No Balm in Gilead 85

Knowledge and Thought 91

Section 1

Jim Sweet's Testimony

CHAPTER 1

War and Narrow Escapes From Death

My father was a Pentecostal Pastor and I remember him building a church when I was just but a lad. He worked in the nearby colliery and when that closed down just after the great strike in 1926 he was with almost all the others in the village out of work and on the dole (government benefits) until the Second World War in 1939. It was during this time of unemployment that the church was built. I do not want to go into the details of it for that is my father's testimony not mine.

When it was opened I found myself having to go there three times on a Sunday, morning service at 11.00 a.m., Sunday school at 2-3 p.m. and evensong service at 6.00 p.m. I had two brothers and a sister who had all given their lives to Christ. I am afraid I was the black sheep of the family. I resented the fact that I had to go to church while my friends were out playing cricket or football. By this time I had reached the age of 21, it was 1939 and we were at war with Germany. I remember the postman delivering a letter addressed to me. I opened it and discovered they wanted my help to win the war. Here was my escape from church three times on a Sunday and twice in the week.

I had to report to a centre in Newport for a medical examination and I had a problem. When I was 10 years old I had an accident with my left eye which was cut right across, as a result I was almost blinded, there was no way I would pass the medical with one good eye. I could see things but it was just a hazy shadow. While I was waiting my turn I memorised the letters on the wall chart so I was able to say I could read them with my left eye. I don't think the doctors believed me but he passed me A1 fit. A few days later I was in the army and I felt as free as a bird.

After about six months I was made a Lance Corporal in the Signal Platoon where I learned to send messages by flag, semaphore and the Morse code. After about 10 months there came a Captain to the Battalion asking for volunteers for a special mission. I think nearly half the company volunteered including me. He interviewed us all but he chose only four of us. Within a few days I was on my way to Manchester where an army truck took us to Sharston.

As a special unit we were encouraged to wear civilian clothes when off duty. Daily we assembled on Brownlie Road and marched to the Aerodrome, later to become Manchester Airport. We at that time were called the No. 2 Commandos. After a few weeks we spent a few months training at Fort William in Scotland where we lived in a large house called 'Forecastle' by the Caledonian Canal. When we returned to Manchester our headquarters was a hut close to the Sharston Hotel on the Stockport, Altrincham Road. There we were no longer known as No. 2 Commandos but as No. 11 Battalion SAS. We continued to train at the Airport and from there made a number of parachute jumps. It was there we gave a display of parachuting for the Prime Minister Winston Churchill. After moving to Chesterfield we finally arrived at Rulford camp near Salisbury where we gave another display for the King and Queen and the two princesses, Elizabeth and Margaret. Our name was changed to 1st Battalion Parachute Regiment.

A week or so later having given a display for the Royal Family we took off for an exercise south of Salisbury. This was a day I will never forget. After jumping from the door of the plane the first thing you feel is the wind from the propellers. Next you feel a slight tug and you know the parachute has pulled out of its bag and the cord which held it to the plane had snapped freeing you to parachute your way to the ground. I thought everything was okay until I noticed I was falling faster than any of the others. I looked up and saw I had a Roman Candle, that is, my parachute never opened and from the ground it would look as if it was a giant candle. IT WAS THEN I PRAYED THE FIRST REAL PRAYER IN MY LIFE. It was the shortest too, "LORD HELP ME." He did and I felt a voice say to me put your hands on those rigging lines and push out. I did with sweat pouring down my face, I looked up to see the parachute opening and then I felt a jerk as it fully opened and stopped my fall. The next second my feet were on the ground and it was the easiest landing I had ever made. Had the Lord delayed for one or two seconds it would have been too late, in a few hours I would have been in a coffin. Yet, experience has taught me that the Lord is never too late in answering our prayers. Did the Lord answer my prayer? Not so much mine but my parent's prayer that God would save my soul. He gave them that assurance so I couldn't die until He had fulfilled His promise to save me. THIS WAS MY FIRST ESCAPE FROM DEATH.

Finally, after a lot of hard intensive training we boarded a train for Glasgow where we boarded a ship which sailed somewhere unknown to us. We stopped at Gibraltar for a day then on to Algiers where we disembarked. From there we marched approximately 12 miles to Maison Blanche Airport from where the Battalion flew into Tunisia and parachuted into a small place called Souk El Arba

The war had now begun in earnest for us and I had now been promoted to Sergeant. Under the command of an officer my platoon was given the job of reconnoitring a hill held by the enemy. During our time there the officer was badly wounded in the leg. I gave the orders for the platoon to make their own way to our lines while I and two others would help the Officer back. We reached the bottom of the hill when to my surprise the Officer ordered us to leave him and return to the top of the hill and hold it at all costs. I said; "but sir we have done the job we were asked to do and we should go and report our findings to the Commanding Officer." It was of no use however, he ordered us back up the hill. We reached the top and sat down. A few minutes later we could hear the enemy creeping past us. They were between us and the way back to our lines. I carried a Sten gun which because of dust would not fire, it was useless. I also had a hand grenade; one of my men had a rifle and the other a pistol. Just then a German Officer stood up and said, "Come and surrender and I will deliver you." I knew what that meant and that really frightened me. Taking the grenade I threw it at him.

They all dropped down seeking cover and while they buried their heads I said to my two soldiers; "Come on" and we ran down that hill and jumped over the Germans and reached a Wadi[1] that was about 15 feet deep and ran to the bottom of the hill. As we were diving into it two or three machine guns opened fire on where we had just run from standing but they were

---

[1] Arabic Origin-a valley, ravine, or channel that is dry except in the rainy season. Google dictionary.

too late we were fifteen feet down in the valley. I haven't explained very clearly all that happened however, THAT WAS MY SECOND ESCAPE FROM DEATH, we made it back safely to our own lines.

A few days later, I with other Sergeants were called to the CO for a meeting to plan an attack on the enemy position I had been reconnoitring a few days earlier. I learned now I was given the job of leading the Battalion up the hill to the enemy's position. When I enquired why I was chosen the answer was simple, "because you know the way".

At about 3.30 a.m. we started out and about 20 minutes later we were halfway up the hill when a 'runner' came from the CO telling us to stop and wait for the zero hour of 4.0 clock before we began our advance into the enemy position. At 4.0 clock, having received the command to move forward, I stood on my feet with my platoon and I hadn't walked but a few paces when a machine gun opened fire on us about 30 yards to our left. It was almost impossible for the gunmen to miss me, yet I got through a hail of bullets without a scratch. THAT WAS MY THIRD ESCAPE FROM DEATH.

I was beginning to feel that there was someone watching over me and only after a few minutes later I had confirmation of that. We reached the top of the hill and started to walk along the crest of the hill when my foot caught in the roots of a bush and I fell headlong into a trench that was about 2 feet 6 inches deep. At that same moment a machine gun opened fire at where I had been standing but in the trench I was safe. I ask you, who could have arranged to trip me up and save my life at exactly the right moment? That was twice in but a few minutes, MY FOURTH ESCAPE FROM DEATH.

It wasn't over yet, however. I led my platoon around the left flank of the enemy and was getting into a position behind them. I began moving up the hill and I looked behind me but the troops were lying down and fearful of going any further. Before you start thinking the wrong things I could sympathise with them for fear is a natural thing in these circumstances. I shouted at them to get up and follow me and then it happened; the enemy had spotted us and hurled grenades at us, a piece of shrapnel went clean through my nose and I was covered in blood. I was dragged down to safety. I felt the bag on my back was rubbing me and making me sore and when I took it off I found a piece of shrapnel had entered my back behind my spine and that was bleeding profusely. Some had also gone through my thigh and taken a piece out, more blood.

A couple of years ago, while I was in hospital, a doctor saw the hole in my nose and he asked me how it happened. I told him and he said if it had been a fraction of an inch further back I would have died. THAT WAS MY FIFTH ESCAPE FROM DEATH. After being transferred from one hospital to another, I finally arrived in Algiers from where I was sent back to England.

I arrived at Hardwicke Hall where I was stationed and after a few days I was again transferred this time to Olay Cross and finally to Albany Barracks on the Isle of Wight. There I worked in the Captain's Quartermaster office being responsible for equipping and clothing a 1000 intake a month (that is new recruits). I remember an intake was about to arrive in a couple of days and I discovered that I was short on some items of clothing. I rang the transport office and ordered a small pick-up truck and driver to take me to the Ordnance Depot at Sandown to collect them. On the way I urged the drivers to go faster because I did not have much time.

We were going at least 60 miles an hour and I remember there was a hill in front and I saw a large lorry parked on the side. As we ascended the hill the sun appeared over the top and shone through the dirty windscreen and almost blinded us. I noticed the driver fall away from the side towards the middle and I assumed he had seen the truck but he hadn't and we crashed into the lorry on my side of the truck. I was flung out and landed on my feet in the gutter on the other side of the road. I looked around and saw that our truck had overturned and pinned the driver underneath. The truck was a total ruin. All I suffered was a sprained ankle. How I escaped with my life was a miracle. THIS WAS MY SIXTH ESCAPE FROM DEATH.

People tell me I was lucky but I tell them it was God answering the prayers of my father and mother and yet through all this I was still unsaved but God had His hand on me.

In the spring of 1946 I was demobbed from the army and I arrived in Congleton, Cheshire where my wife lived with her parents. As a youth the place where I received my final education having passed the exams which gained me a place there was the Abersychan Mining and Technical Institute as we were being trained to be mining engineers. The head there held Bible reading and prayers every morning and he insisted that we learn not just verses but chapters from the Bible. I already knew much of Shakespeare and other poet's works. I delighted my mother-in-law by reciting the poets and the Bible.

One day two men came to the house and asked my mother-in-law if she knew anybody who would teach at Sunday school. "Oh Yes." she said, "my son-in-law would make a good teacher, he knows the Bible by heart." By this time, however, my wife and I had got our own home which was almost a mile away. A week later on Saturday morning they knocked on my door. They said they were looking for a Sunday school teacher. I said;

"Well I haven't got any." They said; "Your Mother-in-law said you would make a good teacher." They asked me if I would go down tomorrow (Sunday). My whole body was revolting at the idea and I tried to make my excuses but the only thing I could say was, "alright I'll come down."

When they had gone I said to my wife Joyce, "I'm not going down," but she said; "You are".

I was stumped, so I got a story about 'Zacheus up the tree' ready. The following morning I arrived at the Sunday school and I was given a class of lads. The Superintendent said, "before you go to lessons I will tell you a story." And that story was Zacheus up a tree. Then we went into classes and I said to the lads "that man has pinched my story, never mind I'll tell it another way." I hadn't been speaking for more than a few minutes when my conscience overtook me and I said to myself, "Jim Sweet, you are trying to tell these children something you don't know yourself." Convicted by my own conscience I got up and ran out of the church, and although it was all uphill I ran all the way home. Going through the back entrance I passed my wife who was preparing dinner and I went straight upstairs and knelt by my bed and pleaded with God to forgive me.

With tears streaming down my face I knew He had forgiven me. I went downstairs and told Joyce what I had done, that I had surrendered my life to Christ. She said, "Oh, but it's not for me." However, that is another story which Joyce will have to tell you. At work the following day, I was telling fellow workmen what I had done and strangely enough I did not receive any adverse comments or mockery.

What I had started then I have dedicated my life to, winning others to Jesus and God has been faithful in using Joyce and I to win hundreds of souls for His Kingdom.

CHAPTER 2

Making a New Start

After my conversion I immediately joined the church where I found the Lord. I continued teaching in the Sunday school and eventually became a Sunday school Superintendent. Shortly afterwards, I was invited to be one of the church leaders also taking on the job of choir master. That involved training the children, also a mixed choir of men and women, plus a male voice choir. During all this time my wife Joyce came to church with me but she never surrendered her life to God. After some years I started taking Bible studies with the young folks and I was asked to preach. Besides preaching in my own church, I was also invited to preach at other churches and this went on for almost 12 years. During this time we also became caretakers of the church living in the house attached. So we were fully occupied in ministry and by this time Joyce had given her life to Christ.

One night, at the church Bible study we were studying Acts chapter 2. Now, as a lad I was brought up in a Pentecostal church, of which my father was the Pastor so I was well acquainted with the chapter. During our discussions I mentioned that we too could be filled with the Holy

Ghost (Spirit) evidenced by speaking in other tongues. I was warned by one of the elders not to preach or mention this as I would be shown the door. However, several of the brethren showed interest. The following Sunday the Elder who had warned me came to the morning service, his face was all aglow with a broad smile and he said to me; "Jim I have got it." I knew immediately what he had got and then he told me someone had lent him a book on being filled with the Holy Spirit and he got on his knees and asked God for this wonderful gift and God graciously answered his prayer.

I was angry with God. I asked Him what He was doing. I said, "Lord, I brought this teaching into the church and you have given him the baptism of the Holy Ghost before me." One night during the week, my wife went to visit her sister who lived a couple of hundred yards away and my lad was out playing with his friends so I decided to go up to my bedroom and ask the Lord to fill me with the Holy Ghost also. I must have been on my knees for over an hour pleading with God. Eventually, I got up and started to go down the stairs and on every step I sat and prayed and pleaded with God to fill me with the Holy Ghost. I remember there were 14 steps down those stairs and I sat and prayed on everyone, still He did not answer me. Then I reached the step at the bottom and prayed again. Before I knew it God filled me on that last step and I burst out speaking in other tongues as the Spirit gave me utterance. I was laughing one minute and crying the next, I was so thrilled that I could not contain myself.

After this experience there was a new dimension not only to my living but to my preaching and witnessing. As a result people, through my ministry, were coming to know Christ as their Saviour. I started to train the young men in my Bible class to become preachers also. I remember on one occasion I gave one young man a very brief outline of a sermon and told him to "put some meat on the outlines" and next Sunday night you can preach it. The Sunday came and his sermon only lasted ten minutes or so but then he stepped down from the pulpit and knelt at the communion rail. I stood up and made an appeal for people to accept God's offer of salvation and seven people stood up and came forward and surrendered their lives to Christ.

The result of all this upset certain members of the congregation and they went to the minister and complained that the services were getting worse than the prayer meetings and that there was no need to find Christ in church. Apparently he agreed with them because a few days later he came to the church and banned me from preaching. In short he would be most happy if I left.

The New Start

That night I left the church and met some of the young people on the way out. They were expecting me to hold class but when I told them I was forbidden and was now leaving the church they picked up their Bibles and left with me. After only two days of leaving two men paid me a visit and said they had heard I was leaving and they asked me if I would join them. Then I said something in reply that astonished me even as I was saying it. "No," I said. "I am going to build my own church." Where that reply came from could only have been inspired by God because I had never dreamt of such a thing.

We started meeting in our homes but all the while praying for a building of our own. In the meantime one of our young ladies, who worked in a solicitor's office, told her boss of our plight. He was an important person in the Masons and he arranged for us to have the use of the Masonic Hall all day on Sundays and two evenings in the week and for this we paid a nominal rent of £1 per day.

The first years we were in the hall the Lord added His blessing and every Sunday almost without exception we saw a soul saved. If we missed a Sunday without this happening the Lord made up for it by saving two the following Sunday. The first year there were over 50 who gave their lives to Christ. The greater part was young people and our Sunday school grew to over a hundred. On occasions I would say to them, I am going into the back room to pray and if any of you would like to come tell your teacher when we go to classes so they know where you are. I have been to many prayer meetings in many different churches but I have never ever experienced the thrill I had of praying with those young people. The room was full of young folk praying that God would save their mothers and fathers and the sincerity and fervour of their prayers brought tears to my eyes. I would give all I have to experience those days again.

Sunday was a busy day with three services, morning, afternoon and the evening gospel service. We brought many of the elderly and children in by mini-bus and also took them home at each service. Consequently, we hardly had time to eat in between but despite this we enjoyed every moment of the day.

I remember one Sunday morning we had a missionary, from the Republic of Formosa, to preach. We started the service with a hymn and before we had got halfway through it the presence of God came upon us and we were all, the whole congregation, standing with our hands raised to heaven speaking in other tongues and praising God. This went on for almost an hour and a half. I turned to the speaker, Rodney Morgan, to say he would not be speaking this morning and he wasn't there! I looked around the room for him and found him standing facing the wall at the back of the room with his hands stretched up the wall. I said; "who are we to speak when God is speaking to His people? Who are we to interrupt God?" I closed the meeting with some difficulty and Rodney came to me,

MAKING A NEW START

his face beaming and said; "I have never been in a service like this before, it has been so wonderful." He was so excited he rang his father-in-law in America and told him that he must come over and visit us. His father-in-law was the Pastor of a large church in America. He did come to England and stayed over a week preaching the gospel every night.

He was terrific and even now 40 years later I can remember his sermons. On leaving us to return home to America he tried to persuade me to go with him because he said I would have greater scope for my ministry. I would not leave my own church because I knew that was where God wanted me.

While using the Masonic Lodge, we purchased a mini-bus and as a result our Sunday school grew enormously. Many adults found Christ and we increased in numbers but I am going ahead of my story.

The week before we were shown the door at the old church I had booked two Pastors to speak at an evangelical service I held once a month. They were due the following weekend. Now I had a problem with no church to invite them to and no congregation. There was just my wife and I and the lads that came out of the old church with us and the wife of one of them. We got together and booked Congleton Town Hall for the event. When we went to book it I said, "If one sits here and one over there the six of us might appear as a reasonable congregation." The Friday night before the service we held an all night prayer meeting that lasted from 8.00 p.m. on Friday night until 6.00 a.m. Saturday morning. On Saturday half an hour before the service I stood at the entrance of the hall. I looked down the road towards the town centre and there was quite a crowd of people walking up to where I was. I looked across the road and many people were coming down Canal Street. I looked to my left and there were many people coming from that direction too. I wondered where these people were going. The next thing they were all passing me and entering into the Hall. That night we had a congregation of over 500 souls. Our average congregation for one of these services in our old church would have been 50 or 60 and all this happened without any advertising whatsoever.

The speakers arrived early, one was a nationally known speaker, J. Nelson Parr, founder and Pastor of Bethshan Tabernacle Manchester, and the other well known speaker was Ernest Sharman of Denton, Hyde. I led the service and the blessing we received that evening became the talking point for the fellowship for weeks. God really answered prayer and our faith in Him grew tremendously. It was at this service that Jean, who eventually became our daughter-in-law, gave her life to Christ. The offerings given at the service were more than sufficient to bless the speakers and pay for the hire of the hall.

WITH SUCH A GOD AS THIS, WHO WOULDN'T TRUST HIM IN THE FUTURE WHATEVER THE NEED?

CHAPTER 3

The Call to Build a Church

As wonderful as the experiences were at the Hall, the call to build our own place of worship was still uppermost in my mind. As a result we went around the town of Congleton searching for vacant ground. The first place we visited was Nursery Lane. It was a large piece of ground, almost an acre. Also it was close to a housing estate which was ideal. I remember walking onto it and a text from Deuteronomy 11:24 came to me. *"Every place where the soles of your feet shall tread shall be yours."* I walked all over that ground and claimed it in the name of Jesus but there were discouragements in the way that would test our faith to the full. There were also many opportunities to believe I might have got it wrong. When we enquired at the Town Hall we received discouragement for they said that the ground had been promised to another church to build a youth centre on it.

I will say this, the Congleton Council Officials did all they could to assist us. They offered us ground at several places around the town. One particular piece of land they offered us was for a nominal rent of a shilling per annum. Our faith was really put to the test but we refused their every offer because we still believed that the Nursery Lane site was the only place.

Several weeks later, one of our members was in conversation with someone from the other church. They no longer required the ground because the government had released their own building back which they had requisitioned for use as a school during the war. Upon receiving this information I went back to the Town Hall and saw the Mayor. When I asked him for that Nursery Lane site he said, "Of course you can have it, I have seen what you have done in collecting the children and taking them to Sunday school and then taking them home again in your mini-bus. Yes you can have it."

Faith in God's Word triumphed again but more testing of our faith was on the way.

Building The Church

I asked Howard Dean, our treasurer, what funds we had and he said we had £350. We purchased the mini-bus for £200 which left us with £150. We needed that bus because our Sunday school had grown to over 100 young people. We purchased the ground at Nursery Lane for £100. The next thing we did was to employ someone to level a part of the ground with a digger. Then we put the foundations in and started building. Where the money came from to buy the bricks and timber I do not know. Looking back it seems strange that I never gave money a thought. We never asked for any, we never borrowed any and yet we paid our way. Only God could have arranged this.

When we do what God wants us to do it is He who will find the

THE CALL TO BUILD A CHURCH

wherewithal to do it if we trust Him. To begin with the architect and the lawyer gave their services for free. This was done voluntarily, we never asked them. The plumbing was done free, a local business man, who was a Christian came to see us and asked what kind of heating we were having and we said it would probably be electric to which he replied; "I will supply that." When we came to paint the church one of our young girl's father was a painter and decorator. We asked her to ask if he could give us some advice. He came and said he would supply the paint if we let him do the entrance hall himself. When we completed the work and asked him for his bill he said; "NO CHARGE." He said, "I have seen you all working yourselves to death and counted it a privilege to be part of that effort." His services and paint were all free.

The grass on the field around had not been cut for years so we could not allow cars to be parked as there might have been holes and obstacles in the ground. A few days before our opening we were still finishing off inside when a man and his wife came from a neighbouring church to look around the building. He said to me; "I can't do anything like this but I can cut grass." He went home and brought his family with scythes and reaping hooks and in a few hours had cleared all the grass away completely. That left us with ample parking for the opening on Saturday night.

Again, let me say when we are doing HIS WILL HE PROVIDES FOR EVERY NEED. So when He caused me to say previously, "I will build my own church" that became a reality. At its completion we did not owe a penny. Praise the Lord!

The church was full with people standing around outside at the opening service. I barely took part in the opening I had invited Charlie Harthern, a pastor who I highly esteemed to lead the service. He persuaded me to take my wife Joyce, for a short holiday as a break from the continued work we had been doing. As wonderful as the opening service was the Sunday morning service is one I shall never forget.

While we had been holding services in the Masonic Hall, Joyce and I always arrived 30 minutes early to tidy up and set out the chairs and light two heaters which we brought to warm the room up. We were always the first there. On the Sunday morning after the opening of the church the night before Joyce and I arrived early as usual to open the church like we had always done in the Masonic Hall. We got out of the car and even as we were walking towards the church we could feel the presence of God. When we arrived at the door we found it was already opened and as we passed through the entrance hall we saw the congregation was already in and the whole congregation was either praying or praising God with their hands raised to heaven. Before I took two or three steps down the aisle the power of God fell on me and I was speaking in other tongues and praising God. That scene continued from 10.30 a.m. until after midday. There was no possibility of me speaking even if I wanted to. How could I intervene when God was speaking to them? I had some difficulty in closing the service but that was necessary for the children who would soon be coming in for Sunday school.

The old bus which we had purchased did a splendid job of bringing the children. The teacher's task was to bring them to the knowledge of Jesus Christ as their personal Saviour. I am glad to report that many of those young ones gave their lives to Him. Soon we had over 100 children in the Sunday school and they so enjoyed it that many of them came to other services too. When we went to other churches on a Saturday evening to support their special events the younger ones insisted on going, so the bus was always full when we travelled.

THE CALL TO BUILD A CHURCH

A group of the older girls took up playing the tambourine. They were trained in the proper use of the instrument by Pastor Albert Garner's wife Peggy. So proficient were they that during one Easter service at Bethshan Tabernacle, Manchester Pastor J. Nelson Parr invited them to play. The witness of the young ones caused many of their parents to give their lives to Christ. It wasn't long before the church was full and we had to extend it to find room.

After being its Pastor for over 14 years I felt my job there was completed and at the invitation of Pastor Phillip Powell of Droylsden, I joined him as co- Pastor. We spent a profitable two years there. We eventually moved to Radcliffe Tabernacle where God blessed our ministry with many souls won for Him. During the eight years we were there the Sunday school grew and also many gave their lives to Jesus (including Barbara Payne and Dennis Rigg). It became a thriving church but at the age of 65 I retired. The business of working for my living and running a church became too much. I had done this for over 25 years. It was only because I had such tremendous support from my wife Joyce that I was able to continue for so long. She was such a blessing amongst the young ones. It was through her ministry the Sunday school grew to over 100.

CHAPTER 4

The Call to the Full Gospel Business Men's Fellowship International (FGBMI)

I soon discovered that the Lord had other ministry for me so there was to be no rest. This time, however it was not to be preaching but giving my testimony.

The first place I was invited to was at the Workington Chapter of the FGBMI. A very good friend of mine Dennis Rigg accompanied me and gave his testimony. There were about 80 at the meeting and from the start there was an excellent spirit in the meeting. When I made the appeal seven people came forward and gave their lives to Christ and many others came out for prayer.

The next month I was at the Ealing Chapter, London, where an airline pilot and a university graduate surrendered their lives to Christ. Here three Catholic ladies, who had been thrown out of Westminster Abbey for criticising the church, came out for prayer also.

A few weeks later I was invited to open a new chapter at Salford and there were many Roman Catholics in the meeting and three gave their lives to Christ. A young man from the Wigan Chapter of the FGBMI came out for healing as a car engine which was being repaired, fell on to his hand and crushed it. The result was he could not move or bend his fingers. He was so upset because he could not play his guitar. I sensed the presence of God to heal so I did not pray for him. I just said; "In the name of Jesus close your hand," and he did "now open it again," and he did. He went all around the room showing his hand to everyone. The next time I saw him he was playing his guitar in the band and he came forward to testify of his healing.

A week later I was speaking at the Stockport Chapter where there were further decisions for Christ. Here a lady was healed of back trouble and for a bonus her neck which she had been unable to turn was released and she went home rejoicing.

On to Blackburn a fortnight later where three surrendered to Christ. A few weeks later saw me at the Bolton Chapter where another three gave their lives to Jesus. Here also Dennis Rigg who had come with me was healed of sciatica. From here Dennis and I, two weeks later, were invited to Newby Bridge. When they knew I was going to Ireland to witness, and this was when the IRA were causing killing and destruction, they took me into an anteroom and prayed for me. This I greatly appreciated. Unfortunately there were no unsaved in the meeting, nevertheless a lady who had been involved in spiritualism was delivered and she returned unto the Lord.

On the 28th March 1988, after a 200 mile journey, I arrived to speak at the Civic Hall in Trowbridge, Wiltshire. Here everything was done decently and in order and the meeting was very subdued and respectable. Nevertheless the presence of God was very real and there was a lovely atmosphere in the meeting and the prim starchiness soon left and the people began praising the Lord. There were two decisions for Christ and almost 50 people came out for prayer. The atmosphere was electric. Then it was back to Lancashire to Wigan where three decisions were made for Christ. It was at this meeting the man who God healed his hand gave his testimony. As a result over 40 people came out for prayer for their families. A young girl called Sylvia sobbed her way to repentance and then made a public confession of her salvation.

A week later I was speaking at a Women's Aglow meeting in Middleton where again there were two decisions for the Lord. Three weeks later I was at Carlisle where God blessed us with the salvation of a young woman who had indicated she wanted to give her life to Jesus. Over 50 people came forward to pray for their families to find the Lord.

On June 6th I was in Ireland and the first meeting was at Ballymena where I was warmly welcomed. Unfortunately there were no unsaved present but about 25 asked for prayer for their families. Before the meeting began I was warned not to mention I had been in the Parachute Regiment as there might be someone from the IRA in the meeting and they feared for my life. From there to Craigavon, Enniskillen, Belfast, Bangor and Donegal but in all these places there were only a few decisions for Christ. There seemed to be no unsaved at all in the meetings but we had some great fellowship in the Lord.

August saw me back home and speaking at the Beswick Chapter then on to Cardiff with Geoff Read where there were four decisions and then on to the Hull Chapter.

On December 5th 1988 Joyce and I were in Inverness and there we met the President of the Chapter Hugh Fraser and his wife Cath. There were five ministers present in the meeting, one a minister to deep sea fishermen, stood up and confirmed what I had said about my father during my early life. He came from a town quite close to where I used to live and he said he knew my father. Fancy meeting someone 500 miles away from South Wales who knew my family? Another stood and confirmed my parachuting for he had been a paratrooper himself. Two people gave their lives to Christ. It was here that the wife of our host Cath Fraser was healed of leg problems. From Inverness I went on to Fort William again where I witnessed for the Lord.

In January 1989, I spoke at the Rochdale chapter where there was one decision. Then Oldham, Sale, Barrow in Furness, Manchester Town Hall,

THE CALL TO THE FGBMI

Southport, Warrington, Harrow, Northallerton, Chorley and Wigan where a policeman and a Mormon lady gave their lives to Christ. Then on to Doncaster, Heywood Women's Aglow, Preston, Lytham St. Anne's, Leigh, Anglesey, Alsager, Wolverhampton and it was at Wolverhampton that a lady who was confined to a wheelchair with arthritis was completely healed.

It was after I left that she got out of her chair and walked around. A couple of months later I was speaking at Lichfield but before I spoke a lady came forward and gave her testimony of healing. She said she was the lady from the Wolverhampton meeting I had not known anything about her healing until that moment. Next I was in Kendal where I received another surprise. After making an appeal for salvation one responded and then I asked if anyone needed prayer for healing. My good friend Eric who had accompanied me on many occasions was with me. Nobody responded when I invited them forward for prayer for healing. I was just about to say "Thank God for a healthy congregation" when a man asked if he could speak. I agreed but what another shock I was going to have.

Some months ago he said I prayed for him at the Bolton chapter, he had come into the meeting on two walking sticks helped along by two brethren one on each side. That night he said after you had prayed for me I threw away my sticks and I have been walking ever since completely healed. I never saw that happen because I had to leave and take some friends home, I was shocked to learn that. Suddenly, the hall became full of sick people after hearing his testimony and I was praying for people until very late into the night.

I was back again at Bolton, Buxton and Leigh, then on to Nottingham where a Jewish lady gave her life to Christ.

Months ago I stopped recording the number of people who had found Christ through my ministry because somehow I didn't think it was right BECAUSE IT WAS THE LORD WHO SAVED THEM, I was but His servant.

There were numerous other towns I witnessed for the Lord including Leeds, York, Newtown, and worldwide Christian Radio Centre, Halifax, Bethshan Tabernacle, Melton Mowbray Warwick and many more.

None of this would have been possible without the tremendous support from my wife Joyce who stayed at home alone waiting for my return which was sometimes the middle of the night. I have thanked God many times for her prayers and support. Thank God for a godly wife. I also had the support of Brother Eric Hanson who testified on many occasions of his wonderful salvation. He was a great help and on our way to meetings he would pray for God's blessing upon us.

Besides all this I was persuaded by Dennis and Barbara Rigg to start Bible studies in my home and I am pleased to record that these studies lasted almost 20 years. I was 86 years old when I finally retired from that.

Joyce and I have served the Lord for 59 years and this while working for my living. Of this I am sure, God is no man's debtor. In my life of service for Him we have seen hundreds of souls won for the Lord and many sick people healed. I would say without hesitation that serving God is not only rewarding but the most satisfying occupation.

Jim and Joyce went home to be with the Lord within weeks of each other in the year 2010.

Section 2

Jim Sweet's Sermons

SERMON 1

Four Stages of Life

JOHN 11:35
"Jesus wept."

There is an ascending sequence of Life. There is LIFE itself. Secondly, there is ABUNDANT LIFE. Then there is RESURRECTION LIFE. This is a life that is submitted to Christ. Those that can say, *"It is no longer I that liveth but Christ that liveth in me,"* (Galatians 2:20) are partakers of the resurrected life of Jesus.

This is a sharing of the life beyond the grave in which one can confidently say, *"O death where is thy sting, O grave where is thy victory."* (1 Corinthians 15:55) A life, in which death has been swallowed up in victory, a life in which the sting of death has been rendered innocuous (or harmless) there is no fear of death. We have already passed from death unto eternal life. The resurrection life then is a life that is lived on a different plane to the natural. We are living in an entirely different realm whose inhabitants are different.

It is in the power of the Resurrection Life that we wage war against the enemy that exists at this level, for in this realm *"we wrestle not against flesh and blood but against principalities, against powers, against rulers of darkness of this world, against spiritual wickedness in high places."* (Ephesians 6:12) Our resurrection life enables us to wage a successful war on the enemy of our souls. We are more than able to hold our own for our very resistance against him causes the devil to flee from us and we are more than conquerors through Him that loved us. There are many saints who are fearful of the thought of dwelling on this level but I want to assure them that this life, at this level, guarantees for us more power than will be against us.

We are assured of victory but there are those who still shy away from walking on these shores and say they will never be able to overcome the enemy. Those who believe that, align themselves with the ten spies who brought an evil report and saying there were giants in the land and we are as grasshoppers in their sight. However, didn't the Lord make giant killers out of Caleb and Joshua and didn't He out of David? Also, the God of Caleb, Joshua and David is our God today.

Maybe you are still quivering in your shoes and think you will lose out, to you Paul threw out a challenge. *"Who shall separate us from the love of Christ, for I am persuaded that neither death nor life, nor angels, nor principalities nor powers nor things present nor things to come nor height nor depth nor any other creature shall be able to separate us from the love of God which is in Christ Jesus?"* (Romans 8:37-39)

A study of these verses will show that everything and everyone outside you are unable to separate you. The only person who can separate you, IS YOURSELF.

Now resurrected does not mean ascended therefore in the natural we are still earthbound, even as the children of Israel were when they occupied the Promised Land which was the earnest of their heavenly inheritance. Now if the overwhelming power of Israel in the Promised Land was the earnest (intense conviction) of their heavenly inheritance the power given to us by the Holy Ghost in our resurrection life must be an earnest of our heavenly power where we shall be more than conquerors through Him that loved us. This very thought is mind blowing, the power we shall have in heaven as kings and priests is the power given to us down here, now in our resurrected lives… that is Spirit filled lives. Doesn't this tremendous thought make you want to join those already on resurrected ground?

Those Israelites too, found the Promised Land full of the enemy as we do and there were those who overcame and those who faltered and those who fell by the way. Assuredly, to the overcomers it is indeed a land flowing with milk and honey, with rivers and streams more than enough to make the hearts of its citizens glad.

There are hills, valleys and fertile plains; there is fruit in abundance with those magnificent grapes of Eshcol. It is a place for cattle and sheep and the ruler is the Lord Himself. Let me invite you over into Canaan's fair land for this is like heaven to me. When you arrive as the children of Israel do, bring a memento of your past, your sinful life and place it next to the cross. When your children ask, "What meaneth this?" tell them you should have been on that cross but Christ Himself took your place that you might have this Life. Thank God for life, thank God for the ABUNDANT LIFE. However, let's praise God with all our hearts for the RESURRECTED LIFE because for the child of God there is something better.

Heavenly Life

Paul in his epistle to the Ephesians declares we are seated in heavenly places in Christ Jesus. (Ephesians 2:6) In Him and through Him we can enjoy the heavenly life. At present we are but in spirit but a day is coming when we shall be there in person. In Ephesians 1:3 *"we have been blessed with all spiritual blessings in heavenly places."* We are indeed citizens of heaven and wherever we may be we are taking a little bit of heaven with us. Every blessing that is dispensed in heaven is ours also because although in the physical we don't live there, we are simply God's heavenly outreach into this world because of our status as citizens we are entitled to them.

There is nothing done in heaven that doesn't affect us, there is no enjoyment we can't have, there is no blessing we cannot share for everything He does whether in heaven or on earth it is for our sakes. There are no select bodies in the commonwealth of heaven for we are all equal in His sight, whether Jew or Gentile.

The whole business of salvation has been an affair into which principalities and powers and even angels have enquired to look into. It is through the Church that the complicated, many sided wisdom of God in all its variety and innumerable aspects is made known to angelic rulers and authorities and demon powers known as principalities and powers in the heavenly sphere.

The whole eternal purposes of God are being revealed to every power in the Universe through the Church. What a terrific thought that we poor sinners, saved by grace, in living the heavenly life are enabling God to demonstrate His wondrous plans and purposes to every authority whether good or evil. No wonder Paul says, *"For this reason (seeing the greatness of this plan by which we are being built together in Christ) I bow my knees before the Father of our Lord Jesus Christ... throughout all ages, world without end amen."* (Ephesians 3:14-21)

Then by having LIFE and manifesting the ABUNDANT LIFE to all around us and taking our stand on resurrection ground in living the RESURRECTION LIFE and participating in the heavenly life we are bringing the glory, wisdom, power and the love of God to things in heaven, in earth and things under the earth.

What a privilege! We in Christ have been raised far above all principalities and powers, might and dominions and every name that is named not only in this world or this age but also that which is to come.

PRAISE THE LORD!

SERMON 2

He Lingered

GENESIS 19:16

"And while he lingered, the men laid hold upon his hand, and upon the hand of his wife, and upon the hand of his two daughters; the Lord being merciful unto him: and they brought him forth, and set him without the city."

Have you ever been shopping with someone when something has caught their eye? They stand there gazing at it, then perhaps picking it up, then putting it down, then they will turn away and you say to yourself thank goodness for that but suddenly they turn back again to it and the whole business begins all over again.

So brothers and sisters, don't we feel exasperated and upset while they linger over something they have no intention of buying? We get so impatient with anyone who lingers but I suppose the most that can befall us is that through their lingering we miss a bus or train or some appointment we had to keep.

Let's consider the lingering of Lot, for it was not simply a bus or a train he would miss or even an appointment. His lingering imposed a far greater problem than those things. That very morning the city in which he dwelt, that called Sodom, was to be destroyed to be devastated by earthquake, fire and brimstone. At his side were two angels urging him to flee from the place. Yet, he lingered?

Now, Lot was not a bad man or even simply an unbeliever. No, Lot was a righteous man, a true believer, a real child of God. Yet, he lingered? Maybe if we recall some instances in the early life of Lot we might discover some reasons for his lingering in this terrible sin ridden city.

Early in life he had made a wrong choice. There was a time when Abraham and Lot had lived and prospered together but their very prosperity brought friction and so they resolved to part company. Abraham offered, *"if you take the left hand then I will take the right or vice versa."* (see Genesis 13:9) Abraham, courteous as he was, gave Lot first choice and Lot looking around him saw the well watered plains of Jordan near Sodom. He saw how rich and fertile it was, a good land full of cattle, full of pasture. This just suited his needs and although it was close by the evil city of Sodom he cared little about that.

The men of Sodom were exceedingly wicked and sinful and they would be his neighbours but that mattered little to Lot. That land was good for his flocks and herds and that was of more importance to him than the presence of evil men.

I noticed too that he chose the place by sight and not by faith for there is no record of his asking God for guidance. He thought more of earthly possessions than the welfare of his soul. He chose that which would be of

HE LINGERED

advantage to him in this life and he totally dismissed the advantages of the life to come. So Lot pitched his tent towards Sodom.

Now strange as it may seem the next time he is mentioned Lot is dwelling in Sodom. He left his tent and dwelt in a house in the streets of that town. What or who persuaded him we may never know. Whether it was his wife or family or his own desire matters little, it is a certain fact he dwelt in Sodom without a good cause.

Christians, you can make a wrong choice in life, settle amongst sinners if you so desire but I know of no surer way of losing your own spirituality and eventually your own soul. (Psalm 1) By living among sinners, having your conversations with them, it will not be long before your sense of sin becomes dulled and you are no longer able to discern between good and evil. Consequently, when the call of God comes, threatening judgement because of your condition you will linger. You have become so accustomed to the voice of evil that when God speaks you will barely hear it. You can have the finest house, the highest paid job but if these are hindrances to your spiritual life you are far better off without them.

Lot lingered, so he lost all his possessions, he lost his wife, his children derided him and his end was a most miserable affair. He lost his testimony, no one would believe him. To his son-in-laws we are told, "He seemed to them as one that mocked." (see Genesis 19:14) In other words they are saying, "who believes anything you say?" His end is not recorded in Scripture for a lingerer has no testimony, no witness and invariably they are too late.

I want to tell you a story more serious and more awe inspiring than Lot and the destruction by fire and brimstone of the city of Sodom from which Lot was called to flee. I want to tell you of a day when the grace of God will be taken away. A day when He will call His people home to heaven. We are living in days when lingerers like Lot abound, when people ought to give their lives to Christ for safe keeping but keep putting it off.

The threat that is hanging over civilization is far greater than that which destroyed Sodom and Gomorrah, yet even with this knowledge they linger. Everything points to the end of time, nations are being shaken, moral codes uprooted and restlessness abounds on every hand. Evil men are beginning to hold sway, especially those of the nature of Sodom and the great countdown to the judgement day of God has begun. Just like it did with Sodom when Abraham prayed, if there be 50, 45, 40, 30, 20, 10 righteous souls there for God to spare it, but the countdown came to an end when Abraham failed to find even that number, and Sodom and Gomorrah perished.

We have nearly reached the end of the countdown; the signs are all around us. Jesus is coming to take His people out of the world whose suffering and torment will make Sodom's destruction look more like a picnic party with fireworks. Yet, despite all the signs around, despite the nearness of His approaching judgement, people still linger and say, *"where is the promise of His coming? For since the fathers fell asleep all things continue as they were from the beginning of creation."* (2 Peter 3:4) Everything still goes on as normal; life goes on in the usual way.

"Be warned, the Lord is not slack concerning His promise as some men count slackness, but is longsuffering toward us not willing that any should perish but all should come to repentance and receive eternal life; but the Day of the Lord will come as a thief in the night in which the heavens shall pass away and the elements shall melt with fervent heat, the earth also and

the works therein shall be burned up." (2 Peter 3:9-10)

The countdown has almost reached zero and you are urged to seek the Lord while He may be found and to call upon Him while He is near. This is the third and final warning God has issued. First, it was on Noah's Day when He said He would drown the world and THEY LAUGHED IN HIS FACE FOR THEY HAD NEVER EVEN SEEN RAIN. Right there in the midst God had told Noah to prepare an ark for the saving of their souls but they simply mocked poor Noah.

Surely there came a day when the countdown was almost complete. God had given a warning to Enoch, what revelation He gave him was memorised in his son's name Methuselah, which literally means, "WHEN HE IS DEAD IT SHALL BE SENT." He lived for almost a millennium, thus portraying the long suffering patience of God. Eventually, Methuselah was on his deathbed and God said to Noah come into the ark and He Himself shut the door. Then the rains came. Ah! It would soon pass over they thought and they still lingered but it persisted and the skies grew darker and darker and they ran to the ark but the door was shut, they beat upon it. Sadly, poor Noah had no means of opening it for what God shuts no man can open. The terror that followed is too terrible to contemplate as the screaming subsided as they were swept away in the flood waters.

Again in Lot's day God again brought the lesson home and righteous a man as he was; it needed two angels to bring him to safety.

Now in these last days God has spoken to us by His Son. He has planted an ark of refuge right in the centre of the earth and that ark is the cross of Christ. It is no hole in the ground, it is no concrete emplacement, the Bible says, *"And a man shall be a hiding place from the wind and a convert from the tempest."* (Isaiah 32:2) That man is the Christ of the Cross, and He says: *"I am the door by Me if any man enters he shall be saved."* (John 10:9) In Noah's day they had but one millennium to decide but God has been exceedingly gracious to us. He has allowed us two millennia since the day of His warning at the cross of Christ. We are in the closing days of the second millennium. I urge you to pass through the door and be saved from the wrath to come and two angels will assist your escape. They are known as Goodness and Mercy, (Psalm 23) and following you they will ensure no evil overtakes you.

SERMON 3

Why Did He Love us so? - Just Because!

GALATIANS 2:20
"The Son of God who loved me and gave Himself for me."

Just a dozen words but they convey the greatest drama in the history of mankind. Throughout history there have been great benefactors, great philanthropists, kings and queens of benevolent nature. However, none of them can say that they loved me and gave themselves for me.

The Son of God is unique in that He really loved us and gave Himself for us. The question might well be asked… "Why did He love us?" What was there about us that God Himself loved us so much that it cost Him His life? I have tried to think of myself to see what is in me to love, let alone God. Who can explain why He loved us enough to die for us?

Let me read a few verses from Deut 7:7-8. In these verses we find Moses trying to explain to the people why God loved them. He ends up by giving one of the most delightfully illogical attempts at reasoning that was ever heard.

In later years David gave up the attempt and all he could say was… *"What is man that thou art mindful of him and the Son of Man that thou visitest Him?"* (Psalm 8:4) After that he threw his pen down in utter bewilderment. On the other hand, Moses makes a valiant effort on the reason why God loves us and he ends up saying in effect and what an illuminating saying it is… "The Lord loved you because He loved you." That frankly is the sum of his reasoning. *"The Lord did not set His love upon you, nor choose you because ye were more in number than any other people, for you were the fewest of all people but because...* (It is at this point we wait with baited breath for Moses to give us some dramatic revelation for God's love, but we end up no wiser than before) *...the Lord loved you."* (Deuteronomy 7:7-8) He could get no further than that.

It is undoubtedly the greatest riddle in the universe. André Crouch, the modern gospel song writer, gave an attempt and he could only say… "I don't know why Jesus loved me, I don't know why He cared. I don't know why He sacrificed His life, Oh but I'm glad, I'm glad He did."

Now, if you are hoping that today you are going to hear an explanation of why He loves us, I am afraid you are going to be disappointed. There is no reason in love; it is illogical at the best of times. Someone once said that God was just as delightfully illogical and unreasoning about it as He was when having made the sun to rule by day and the moon by night. In the sheer joy of His heart He dipped His hand deep into His bag and flung the stars about the sky and then laughed as He thought with pleasure on all those who down the long ages would thank Him for the stars also.

David said, "He made the stars also" and let the statement go at that for he could find no adequate reason why God should. After saying that, all I really want to say is, isn't that part of the reason for our reluctance in believing and resting in the love of God. The illogical simplicity of it all?

We think sometimes that God must be dazzled by our size, our importance, our ability, our goodness. What did Moses say to the children of Israel?... *"The Lord did not choose you because you were more in number than any other people."* (Deuteronomy 7:7) He didn't love them because they were mightier and greater than others. That's just the trouble with our faith; we simply can't believe that the prayer of a child by its bedside is of more account than all the galaxies of stars and planets that go swinging around. We think, how can God love us, we are nobodies? Even in the world men pass us by without even the time of day. If you can't see for the life of you that God loves you, or even gives a moment's thought for you then you have hit the very reason He does. He loves you… because.

Jesus gave no reason in His story of the Prodigal Son for the amazing behaviour of his father. That wastrel of a son, that pleasure seeking son, who wasted his substance and who spent all his money, pawned all his goods to spend time on riotous living. That disgrace of a son who had deserted his father and brought shame to his name, who while he was yet a great way off his father saw him, had compassion on him and ran and fell on his neck and kissed him.

WHY DID HE LOVE HIS SON SO? - JUST BECAUSE!

Why did the Good Samaritan, who having done a good turn to the man waylaid by robbers, return in the morning to give the landlord of the inn two pence to pay for the man's keep? He already had done all that could have been expected of him. He did it, just because.

Now, I want you to discover the wonderful intensity of God's love for us. *"For God so loved the World He gave His only begotten son that whoever believes in Him, should not perish but have everlasting life."* (John 3:16)

I want you to notice that God loved us NOT pitied us. If it was only pity, I for one would be utterly disappointed. I read once of a man who married a woman because he pitied her conditions and circumstances. When she found out that he did not love her but only pitied her, it broke her heart; and so it is with us. We like her would sooner be married to the poorest and be loved than to the richest simply for pity's sake. God proved His love for us by what He gave. He gave His only begotten Son, allowed wicked men to work their wicked will on Him. Allowed them to nail Him to a cross and allowed Him to take the responsibility for our sin and pay the extreme penalty, that of death, for us.

WHY? So that we might escape the condemnation ourselves for He took on Him all our sins and God poured out His awful judgement upon Him and not on us. Yes, God so loved me that He gave His only Son to die for me that through His death I might be saved.

Now what about the love that the Son has for us? Our text says, *"The Son of God who gave Himself for me."* (Galatians 2:20) What was involved in the giving of Himself?

In Psalm 22:14 David prophesying of the Lord said, *"I am poured out like water, all my bones are out of joint, my heart is like wax, it is melted in the midst of my bowels."* Now if I were to pour a glass of water on the earth would I ever expect to get it back? No, never!

Here Jesus pours out His body for us. He gave His back to the smiters. They make great weal's on it with the whips. Every bone of His was out of joint. One cannot begin to describe the agony of His sufferings, so great were they. This was the judgement He paid for your sin and mine. Is it any wonder Isaiah confidently declares, *"And by His stripes we are healed."* (Isaiah 53:5) Yes, He gave His body for us.

Isaiah 53:12 says, *"He hath poured out His soul unto death"* but great as His bodily sufferings were, they were nothing compared to the suffering of His soul. He who knew no sin was made sin for us and His soul revolted so much at that experience that it literally broke His heart. Isaiah 53:10 says, *"When thou shall make His soul an offering for sin, He sees the seed."* That is you and I brought into the family of God. Yes, He poured out His soul for us also. Proverbs 1:23 *"Turn you at my reproof, behold I will pour out my Spirit unto you."* It wasn't enough to give His body and soul He poured out His Spirit to us also. To enable us to live the life He won for us by His death.

Well, you may be thinking that is all He can give… body, Soul and Spirit. But no, He did not just die for us, He did not just save us, He did not give His life and leave us without any means of support. No indeed, there was something else He could give. Song of Solomon 1:3 *"Thy name is as ointment poured forth."* Oh the wonder of it all, HE HAS given us His name to use. *"Whatever you ask in My name, I will do."* (John 14:13)

Our every prayer and request is by His name. Ask He said, in My name that your joy may be full. (1 John 1:4) Ask around and find out what value there is in being able to use that name. In times of trouble, in times of doubt, in times of sadness, in times of sickness, in times of despair, in times of joy, that name has brought more comfort, more assurance and more help than 10,000 social security workers.

He's always there when things go wrong. He's always there in times of joy. He's a very present help in time of need. (Psalm 46:1) Yes, He gave us His name too.

Do you understand our text now? The Son of God who loved me and gave Himself for me?

WHY DID HE LOVE US SO? JUST BECAUSE! Amen.

One of Jim Sweet's favourite hymns I remember was '**Love lifted me**'.[1]

> Love lifted me
> I was sinking deep in sin
> Far from the peaceful shore
> Very deeply stained within
> Sinking to rise no more
> But the Master of the sea
> Heard my despairing cry
> From the waters lifted me
>
> Now safe am I
> Love lifted me!
> Love lifted me!
> When nothing else could help
> Love lifted me!
>
> Love lifted me!
> Love lifted me!
> When nothing else could help
> Love lifted me!
>
> All my heart to Him I give
> Ever to Him I'll cling
> In His blessed presence live
> Ever His praises sing
> Love so mighty and so true
> It merits my soul's best songs
> Faithful, loving service, too
> To Him belongs

---

[1] Source: Musixmatch, Songwriters: Howard E. Smith / James Rowe
Love Lifted Me lyrics © Universal Music Publishing Int. Ltd., New Spring Publishing, Inc.

Love lifted me!
Love lifted me! (It was love, lifted me)
When nothing else could help (Nothing else could help)
Love lifted me!

Love lifted me!
Love lifted me! (Yes His love lifted me!)
When nothing else could help
Love lifted me!

When nothing else could help
His love lifted me!
Oh His love lifted me

SERMON 4

Corinthians 1:17

"For Christ sent me not to baptise, but to preach the gospel, not with words of wisdom lest the cross of Christ be made of none effect. For the preaching of the cross is to them that perish foolishness, but unto us which are being saved it is the power of God."

It seems to me that we are living in a day and age when people are looking for great sermons and unless the preacher is a noted one, then they will not stir out of their homes to hear him. Yet, I am convinced in my own mind that most of what we hear are sermons full of the wisdom of men and consequently the cross of Christ has been made of no effect, even as Paul says in our text.

Before a certain preacher got up to minister in one service, prayer was made for him, and that prayer opened with this inspired request. "Oh Lord we thank thee for our brother, now blot him out. Reveal thy glory to us in such blazing splendour that he shall be forgotten."

If that happened every time how great our sermons would be, even the simplest of them? But when the preacher is admired there is no inspiration in the word, they do not reverence God. They appreciate the preacher but they do not repent. They are interested but not exalted. They say, "What a fine sermon!" not "What a great God!" They say, "What a way he has with words" but not *"Oh the depth of the riches both of the wisdom and knowledge of God."* (Romans 11:33)

Oh, that the words of the speaker would reveal only the glory of God until in their minds the congregation loses sight of the speaker and sees only the glory and majesty of Christ being lifted up into heavenly places. The sermon being but a commentary leading them on from glorious views to more glorious views until they are lost in wonder, love and praise. Unfortunately this is not the end we always come to and we feel let down and disappointed. Sadly, the truth of the matter is that too often it is left to the sermon alone to lead us to the glory of God when in fact everything in the service should be an aid in arriving there.

If we would see the Lord high and lifted up then there must be reverence. Reverence in the congregation, reverence in the pulpit. Not necessarily mournful reverence but joyful, a joyful response that we all may be of some help in reaching the desired haven. Too often we use preliminaries as just something to fill the time but if we are to gaze upon heaven everything from the choruses, to the sermon should be instruments to lead us to the throne. Our prayers are vital for it is a fact that if people are unmoved by our prayers they never will be by our sermons. I want you to note this next remark because I believe it is of vital importance.

THERE CAN NEVER BE MORE POWER IN OUR PREACHING THAN IN OUR PRAYERS.

The climax may come in the sermon but the preparation and power can only come on our knees before God. It is there that the way of the Lord is prepared. It is there that the bark of the olive tree has been pierced which causes the oil to overflow in our gatherings together. The oil, which is the Holy Ghost, who only can bring us into the presence of Almighty God. The heights that we reach on our knees will be the heights we reach in our services. God makes each and every one of us a mighty prayer warrior. If but half a dozen of us have been to glory on our knees then that blessing must ultimately manifest itself before the service ends.

We are being encouraged to use this and that method to brighten (enliven) our services but it is not brighter services we need but the overwhelming presence and power of the Holy Ghost.

We are exhorted to make our services more pleasant and our themes more up to date. If they are a little sensational so much the better, for it is true we live in sensational times and we must at least match that. In some respects there may be an element of truth in that for I remember the apostle Paul, who lived in a day of great change, resolved problems by being *"...all things to all men that he might win some"*. (1 Corinthians 9:19) Nevertheless, in all the variety of his relations he never changed his themes.

He moved amid the splendour of Ephesus who boasted the presence of the great goddess Diana, he stayed for a time amongst the philosophers of Athens who worshipped at the altar of the 'unknown God'. He reasoned with the Jews and Greeks in the Synagogues of Corinth. He expounded the Scriptures to members of Caesars' household in Rome. Yet, wherever he went whether it was Lystra or Pamphillia or down by the riverside with that seller of purple Lydia, or witnessing to Felix or Festus or Agrippa, he determined to know nothing among men save Christ and Him crucified. (see 1 Corinthians 2:2)

Like many others I am persuaded that amid all the changed conditions of our day, the social upheavals, the race for wealth and power, the quest for pleasure, we shall gain nothing by pandering to their ways by being light hearted and frivolous in our services.

I am convinced that what the people of our generation need is not something on par with which they are living but the deep abiding things that really matter. They need to know as opposed to their sinful nature, the holiness of God, the love of God, the grace of our Lord Jesus, the wonders of the cross, the ministry of divine forgiveness the power of the resurrection, the heavenly places attainable in Christ Jesus, the endless life, Father's house and the glorious liberty of the children of God.

I tell you friends those headlines are infinitely greater than any found in National newspapers. They are more momentous than all television news and so amazing are their content that no newspaper would print it for fear of ridicule. Yet, to us who are being saved it is the Power of God. It is these themes that are the power of God in a sinful heart. The world is tired of the promises of men; it is hungry for truth. It wants more than a talker, it seeks a prophet. It wants more than a signpost, it wants someone who knows the way to Zion's Hill and who will lead them there in authority born of knowledge of Him WITH WHOM THEY WILL HAVE TO MEET.

Knowledge of His love and compassion, knowledge of His saving grace and a knowledge that a welcome awaits them. Has He not promised that, *"Him that cometh to me I will in no wise cast out"* (John 6:37) Also, to aid us in this task we have the grace of our Lord Jesus Christ and the love of God and the communion of the Holy Spirit and with these as our helpers how can we fail?

SERMON 5

Lifted Up

JOHN 12:32

"And if I be lifted up from the earth I will draw all men unto Me."

It seems to me that this text is used more in relation to the sinner than anything else but that little word ALL means that it incorporates not only sinners but saints.

However, attraction for the sinner is pardon from sin but for us it is the deliverance from the power of sin. As our gaze is riveted on the cross of Christ, we see there in His suffering and sorrow what Holiness really is and we say like Paul, *"Oh wretched man that I am who shall deliver me from the body of this death?"* (Romans 7:24)

For it is certain as we gaze upon Him hanging there we shall be conscious of our guilt. Then as we gaze further upon Him it finally dawns on us, *"There is no condemnation to those who are in Christ Jesus"* (Romans 8:1) and this revelation draws us even closer and again we cry with Paul from the bottom of our hearts, *"That I may know Him and the fellowship of His sufferings."* (Philippians 3:10)

Jesus, hanging there shows us the wonder of His love, voluntarily suffering for the sake of others. To us that is unnatural and we shrink from it and hurry away, yet it goes on in all forms of life. We confess that when we see it, it always excites our admiration, especially when the strong gives its life for the weak.

"For a righteous man one might dare to die." (Romans 4:7) For a great worker, or great thinker, but for the common man, for the weak, the imperfect, the diseased, the ignorant, the foolish, would it not be a waste of a good life?

Is it right that we should imperil our lives for the sake of the worthless society? There is one answer to those who believe that even this sacrifice is worthwhile and the answer is Christ. Scientists and other men of learning are constantly propagating the doctrine of the survival of the fittest they say, "does not even nature teach that?"

However that may be, the world in general still has the belief that the true hero is not the most intellectual nor the richest man but the man who acts entirely on the law of love. Who gives his best service for others and never stops to ask, "Is it worthwhile?" Cast your mind back and think of the times you have said, "It is not worth it!" or "they are not worth it!" Know this, the law of love does not operate on the worth of things, or people, or on any other value but love itself.

The love of Christ is the finest example of this law. He died, just for the unjust. There was no moral worth in any He gave His life for but He loved us and gave His life for us.

When we look at the cross we are amazed at His youth. He was not an old man who was coming to the end of His life; it was only just the beginning.

His life was more fruitful, more precious than any other, yet He gave it for the poor, the weak, the characterless, the backsliding and yes even for the men who were torturing Him. For those who demanded His death, for you and for me and all who have betrayed Him for thirty pieces of silver and very often even less.

All that for us who hated and despised Him and as we hear that last despairing cry and watch His head sink on to His chest, indicating that He had died, we may well up with tears in our eyes gaze upon Him and repeat those wonderful words.

"For the Son of God who loved me and gave Himself for me."

Friends ponder on those wonderful words, *"The Son of God who loved me and gave Himself for me"* (Galatians 2:20) and let them sink into your very soul, until your very heart goes out to Him. Until they draw you to His feet, until they send you forth with a glow in your soul that somehow, somewhere you are going to do likewise.

This power, this desire to do something for others is a divine power and when you have got it, it makes life really worth living. It is not a question of just doing good works; He didn't give His life for us to make us wealthy and comfortable. No indeed, He gave His life that we may have life and that for all eternity. We give our lives that they too may enjoy the wonderful life He has given to us.

The appeal of the cross is to all men, those who care for nothing, those who deny Him, those who trifle with Him, those who despitefully use Him, even the vilest sinners. He looks down from the cross and says, "Yes you are mine." For God commanded His love towards us and while we were yet sinners Christ died for us. His embrace knows no limit and He looks to us and says, "I want you too."

What decision are we making, what single thing are we doing differently because of the love of God? How great is that love which draws us to Himself and when we feel the claim of that love, how poor and miserable our lives seem, how poverty stricken our gifts to the cause of God?

Before we looked at the cross we really thought we were liberal and charitable and even self denying but now we have seen this giving, we are ashamed of our own. It is a certain fact that if once the love of God takes possession of us, it will not let us stop in mere selfish ends or mere observance, in mere church going as an end in itself, or in the mere listening to sermons and going away the same as before. No indeed, it will grip our hearts and souls until it makes us real workers for Him somehow, somewhere and the words He spoke to His disciples will come ringing into our ears, convicting us. If He laid down His life for us, we ought by whatever means to lay down our life for the brethren.

Yes, lay down our lives, die to self, die to self-love and die to self-will for the sake of others. Moved by the love of God that you will not only give your coat but your cloak also, you will not only walk the mile of common courtesy but go the extra mile. Not just simply putting your hands in your pockets but learning for all time the great truth that God can only reach man through man and that He does want man, He wants you, He wants me and all who call themselves Christians in order that through us He might reach the indifferent, the helpless, the hopeless, the unlovable who are outside. That they too might taste of the unsearchable riches of His grace.

Ah! you say, "I can't preach or even teach," maybe not but you can open up your heart, you can influence; you can show them what they don't often see in Christians these days, the loving Spirit of Christ. That is the only influence which will attract sinners. We may build churches; we may read lessons and preach sermons and even pray at times and produce no effect. Christ must be made actual in our lives for as God was revealed in Christ Jesus, so must Christ be revealed in us. When we catch the spirit of the cross then our witness will become great again and that spirit is the laying down of our lives for the brethren.

Let me emphasise this, even in His darkest hour on the cross Christ had no word of reproach, no words of condemnation, no word of bitterness or criticism, nothing but real heartfelt compassionate forgiveness. How much of our lives when we gather together is spent pointing the finger, in harsh unworthy criticism, in pulling to pieces, in degrading the efforts of another instead of encouraging one another, helping those who are weak in the faith. Exhorting those who are weary to keep on and pleading with others who have laid down their arms to take them up again and fight. How often, when we are tired ourselves, do we still go the extra mile and when poverty comes near our door, we have still given our cloak also.

If you feel none of these things move you I ask you to take a look at the cross again. Take a look at those five bleeding wounds, take a look at the love poured out there and cry. "Let it Oh! God flow through me, let Your Spirit of grace overwhelm me, flood my life with Your presence till men and women will cease their searching and find Christ in me the Hope of Glory."

SERMON 6

Humility

EPHESIANS 3:8

"Unto me, who am less than the least of all saints, is this grace given, that I should preach among the Gentiles the unsearchable riches of Christ..."

Romans 12:3 says, *"For I say unto you for the grace given unto me, to every man that is among you not to think of himself more highly than he ought to think."*

How is it that those with the least claim to fame always seek to exalt themselves? I suppose that's because their works do not proclaim their greatness, their tongue has to.

Undoubtedly, one of the finest minds that ever lived was also one of the most humble. The apostle Paul was head and shoulders above his contemporaries and none has reached the fullness of the stature of this man since. He is a prince among men, a giant among pygmies and an intellectual amongst the ignorant. And he says of himself, *"I am least of all the saints."* (Ephesians 3:8)

He had pioneered goodness and God knows how many churches. He had written 14 epistles whose depth of spirituality is still above the finest intellect today. For the Lord's work he laboured night and day or as he said, *"In labours more abundant, in stripes above measure, in prisons more frequent."* Five times he had received 39 stripes, three times he had been beaten with rods, once he was stoned and three times he was shipwrecked besides many other perils of which we can read in 2 Corinthians chapter 11.

This is the measure of the man's fidelity and faithfulness to God. This is his measure of his love to God and yet he could declare, *"I am less than the least of all saints."* (Ephesians 3:8) This is the measure of the man's humility. This is but the account of his sufferings for Christ and of his labours.

Even his 14 epistles will not do him justice, *"I will gladly spend and be spent for you"* and he counted all things as loss for Christ and indeed he had suffered the loss of all things and counted them but dung that he might win Christ and to know the love of Christ which passes all knowledge. (see Ephesians 3 and Phillipians 3)

When I compare him to others, oh! the shame I feel for them but when I compare him to myself, I feel less than a worm. What do I know of the sufferings of Christ? What do I know about the loss of all things for Christ and as I read him further I wonder if there is anything at all in my life that has caused me even a moment of anxiety for Christ?

Then surely, if I have never experienced the hurt, I have never experienced the healing. If I have never experienced sadness, I have never experienced joy. If I have never experienced loss, then I have never experienced the gain.

HUMILITY

Surely his loss was gain. He had lost all things but he had gained Christ and as he says in Colossians 3:11 "And Christ is all," all he ever dreamed about, all that he ever hoped for. Did he want health, did he want peace, did he want joy, did he want life? Then it was all in Christ. The things he had lost could never have purchased one of these. Yes, he had gained. He had given his all and it was returned unto him in a measure *"pressed down shaken together and running over."* (Luke 6:38) But for all this gain he was not puffed up with pride. He never saw himself as a perfect Christian. How many people do we meet who think they are the 'bees knees'? They are past teaching and trying to exhort them is an utter impossibility. They are insulted if you suggest that there are areas of their lives that could be improved or that there was more they could do.

As for renewing their vows, as we so often do, they really believe they are beyond that stage and have reached the age of perfection where there is nothing left for them to do. Yet, in all his majestic greatness, Paul could say, *"I have not attained, nor am I already perfect, I follow after."* (Philippians 3:12) Here was a man who had visited the third heaven, who had a personal encounter with the Lord on the Damascus road and who had founded dozens of churches saying, "I have not attained perfection nor indeed have I reached it but I am following hard after it."

He knew more than anyone the faults and failings of his own life. He realised that unless they were brought under subjection he could become a castaway. One day taking an inventory of his faults and failings he cried, *"O wretched man that I am who shall deliver me from the body of this death?"* (Romans 7:24) I pray that each and every one of us shall seek not so much perfection but humility, for that indeed is the way of perfection. Our prayers should constantly be as the publican's, *"Lord be merciful to me a sinner,"* (Luke 18:13) for we are but sinners saved by grace.

We have nothing of which we can be proud of for we are what we are by the grace of God. It has been said, it is only when we have one foot in the grave that we realise the depths and extent of our sins. Also, I might add it is only when we have one foot in the grave that we realise the poverty of our efforts for Him. It is only when we have one foot in the grave that we realise our lack of love for Him and we begin to tremble lest a voice from heaven thunders, *"I have somewhat against thee because thou hast left thy first love."* (Revelation 2:4)

We have been so proud, so independent that He hardly came into our daily reckoning and when the books are made up we shall find that in our lives He hardly gained a mention and yet He has exhorted us, *"Ye that make mention of the Lord, keep not silent."* (Isaiah 62:6) We are exhorted to make mention of His Righteousness. We are exhorted to make mention of His loving kindness. Having got both feet in the grave and landed in heaven, we shall then be taught the greatest lesson of all, humility. When we shall see Him in all His splendour, when we shall see Him in all His glory, when we shall understand the greatness and vastness of His power, when we shall see the King in His beauty and those awful scars in His hands and side and His feet and realise that it was our sins that did this. Then we shall cast our crowns before Him and fall prostrate at His feet crying, "My Lord and My God."

Then and only then will we understand true humility. Then and then only will we understand Philippians chapter 2; and then and only then will this mind be in us which was also in Christ Jesus. (Philippians 2:5-11)

SERMON 7

Kingdom

MATTHEW 6:33

"Seek ye first the Kingdom of God and His righteousness and all these things shall be added unto you."

Would each and every one of us hang this text in a prominent place in our home and live and abide by its promises? If ever we needed to take a fresh look at this text again it is today when the world in general is in such a state of confusion. When wickedness and evil are considered the normal state of life. This is the day when Christian's peace and joy should shine forth amidst the gloom the NIV gives a better rendering than the King James Version. It translates, *"Take no thought, so do not worry."* (see Matthew 6:25) Yet how many of us day by day are constantly worrying about the simple things of life? If we are so concerned and upset by these what is our condition when faced with the major issues of life?

Listen carefully, in Exodus 15 and 16 the great sin of the Israelites in the wilderness was their murmuring, worrying and anxiety about food, drink and provisions. Their failure to trust God on these minor issues eventually led to their failure to trust God to take them into the Promised Land. Worry is a sin and how many of us are guilty of this? Yet this verse gives the solution for freedom from worry. *"SEEK YE FIRST THE KINGDOM OF GOD AND HIS RIGHTEOUSNESS."* (Matthew 6:33) The emphasis here is laid upon our submission to His authority, that shall truly rule and reign in our hearts. Indeed His every command should be our pleasure to perform. That as Lord and King He should have the preeminence in our lives. That His work should have priority over all personal desires and that God should be first in our lives and there should be unconditional submission to His will.

It is the ones who fulfil these conditions who can with utmost confidence cast their worries and cares on Him and know of a surety that He will care for them. You may be young and unable to earn your own living, you also may be old and infirm and unable for 1000's of reasons to earn your own living. While the young and strong (lions David calls them) do lack and suffer hunger, *"They that seek the Lord shall not want any good thing"* (Psalm 34:10) and again *"Behold the eye of the Lord is upon them that fear Him upon them that hope in His mercy to deliver their soul from death and to keep them alive in famine."* (Psalm 33:19) What a guarantee but a conditional guarantee, conditional upon putting Him and His righteousness first. It is not a guarantee from trouble, trials and afflictions. It is a guarantee from worry and you know and I know that the greatest killer of all is worry. We read of Jesus being hungry, being thirsty and having nowhere to lay His head but we never read that He worried because He didn't.

Hadn't He fulfilled all His Father's demands? Hadn't He spoken only those words which God gave Him? Hadn't He been obedient to His earthly parents and had He not submitted to the baptism of John to fulfil all righteousness? Also having lived a blameless life for 30 years He was tempted in every way possible with Satan himself as the personal tempter. He was tempted on all points such as we are, yet without sin. The three greatest temptations to the Christian are in the World, the Flesh and the devil. John, in his epistle, majors on the attraction of the world and Peter and James on the temptations of the devil and Paul on the flesh.

The first temptation that Jesus endured was of the flesh. He was desperately hungry and the devil tempted Him to command a stone to be made into bread. What was wrong with performing a simple miracle to meet His need? How many of us in a similar situation would jump at the chance, even probably to the extent of saying that it was God who made the opportunity available. When things have bright prospects we always assume we are in the will of God. The temptation to escape our temptation by grasping at immediate blessings is often the greatest temptation we can endure. The temptation of Jesus here was to take a short cut to the meeting of an immediate need but He knew the things of God must come first, however much His flesh longed for satisfaction and blessing. He knew that seeking the Kingdom of God and His righteousness would bring bread afterwards.

How different we are, always wanting the blessing first, always seeking for things to satisfy our desires. Always praying for this or for that when the obvious thing is to seek Him and His righteousness. I can almost guarantee that if the finest preacher in the world was ministering and he went on rather long about the things of God, there would be those who would get up and go home because they were hungry. God help us get our priorities right.

His next temptation was the world. How quickly He could have had the applause of men if He had leapt from the pinnacle of the Temple and came floating down to the ground? The sensational always appeals to the world. Just fancy a legion of angels rescuing Him just before He hit the ground. He would have the applause of the world but that applause would never have glorified God. A miracle simply to pander to the world is a misuse of the power of God. Jesus would never do that.

Finally, the devil tempted Jesus with His own power. The kingdom of the world was in his hands, he had pre-eminence in all the world's affairs. He was the god of this world and it seemed everyone did his bidding and made obeisance to him. The devil offered Jesus the whole kingdom if He would worship him. In other words He would gain the kingdom by sin, by worshiping Satan instead of God.

After a life of perfection He was tried to the limit, for the work He was called to do demanded that in everything complete obedience to His Father's will was necessary. We praise God He came through that test with flying colours and though He went into the temptations FULL OF THE HOLY SPIRIT He returned triumphant in THE POWER OF THE SPIRIT. Before He became our Saviour He had to pay the price. Before He went about doing good and healing all that were oppressed, He had to pay the price. All the things the devil offered Him by default became His by His triumph over temptation and His obedience unto death.

If we want to live the life of triumph then we too must be prepared to pay the price!

SERMON 8

Revival

PSALM 51:12

"Restore unto us the joy of thy salvation."

Very often we use this word in the wrong way. When we see or hear of 100's or 1000's of souls being saved we say there is a revival going on. Actually, what we are seeing or hearing about is not revival but the effects of revival. You cannot revive something that never had life. Therefore revival must be with those who have experienced life but whose life has become dormant. Unfortunately, much of the Church of God is in this state. While we are like this it is impossible to inspire a desire in anyone outside of Christ to seek for life in Him.

To give your church an exciting new name is not enough, the Church of God needs to be revived into an exciting vibrant witness for Him. Lives will then bear testimony of the redeeming grace and the joy and thrills of walking with the Saviour. No worldly life can compare with the excitement and wonder of the Christian life but the truth is the world is displaying more exciting things and has more pleasure to offer than they can see in many Christian fellowships.

We need to cry aloud to God like David in Psalm 51:12 *"Restore unto us the joy of thy salvation."* The days before the Israelites were to leave the wilderness behind and cross over the Jordan to a *"land flowing with milk and honey,"* Joshua said to the people, *"Sanctify yourselves for tomorrow the Lord will do wonders amongst you."* (Joshua 3:5) What a wonderful promise? *"Tomorrow the Lord will do wonders among you."* I can hear someone saying, "Tomorrow never comes," and sadly for many that is the truth. Those Israelites had been wandering for over 40 years in the wilderness. Years and years of wandering if it would ever end, now suddenly there was this promise of an end to those barren years.

Let me remind you that every Pentecostal outpouring of the Spirit is always preceded by preparation. The baptism of the Holy Ghost is always preceded by the baptism of repentance and so with the promise made to the Israelites, God's tomorrow of wonders had to be preceded by TODAY'S SANCTIFICATION. All of God's promises have a condition attached and so if we would see tomorrow's wonders we have to sanctify ourselves today. Put another way; God's tomorrow of wonders and power waits for our today of sanctification. It is also true that we must wait for God's time for revival, we cannot make it come any sooner but it is also true that His time is when the Church is ready for it. It is a mighty miracle the Church needs to shake itself out of its lethargy and oftentimes soul destroying services that have no life in them.

A study of Scriptures will show however that miracles have always occurred in every day and generation. Not a day passes, or has passed, without a miracle taking place. However, the Bible reveals they have been more prominent in times of great crisis. Therefore, there were many miracles in the time of Moses when God's people were in cruel bondage but the miracle that really affected them was the Passover which instigated their deliverance from the bondage of Egypt. This however did not happen until they had their day of sanctification.

There would have been no miracles by God but for that. Exodus 12:28 says, *"And the children of Israel did as the Lord commanded them."* A day of sanctification preceded their deliverance from Egypt's bondage and a day of sanctification preceded their entrance into the Promised Land.

Upon us rests the responsibility of fixing the time of God's display of might and power, for His delay is only because of our unreadiness. Our cry is, "How long O Lord?" or "send it now," and the sad reason why revival doesn't come is that we are not ready for it. Let me assure you the power of God never changes, never varies but the display of His power varies according to the readiness or faithfulness of the Church of God.

Where are the miracles that show God's power today? It seems to me according to Scripture it is impossible to preach a real sermon without the miraculous evidence following it. Does it not say, "Signs and wonders shall follow the preaching of the Word?" (see Mark 16:20) The only miracles however, that are preached today is that man benefits from and which display only the mercy and compassion of God, such as healing or the supplying of our needs. It is sad but true to say that people will accept all God's good gifts but never remember the Giver. The crowds followed Jesus because of the bread which fed them; even His disciples soon forgot the miracle of the loaves and the fishes. Remember too the nine lepers. None, or very few are changed by this type of miracle.

The miracle that does change lives is always the miracle of the judgement of God. It was with Pharaoh and the Egyptians when God slew their firstborn and again on Mount Carmel when the fire from God fell. They soon cried, *"The Lord, He is God!"* (1 Kings 18:39) Remember the judgement of God which fell on Ananias and Sapphira, when they perished at Peter's feet? The Scripture says, *"Great fear (awe) fell upon the people."* (Acts 5:5) When God acts in miracle judgement people tremble, when He acts in mercy they disregard Him.

The reason we don't see the miracle of revival is because we have neglected the principles stated in our text, "Sanctify yourselves." Unbelief has locked the door of the powerhouse and shut fast the door of our hearts. The word 'sanctify' means, put yourselves in the condition and attitude that God, in a moment's notice, can use us. In other words, set yourselves apart from the world with its attractions, from the deadening influence of unbelief, take God at His word and be solely available for Him. Today we think if we sing a few choruses with jazzy tunes we are doing great but during the Welsh revival of 1904 the chorus they sang was, 'Bend me Lower.'

They were obviously well acquainted with 2 Chronicles 7:14, *"If my people who are called by my name shall humble themselves and pray, and seek my face and turn from their wicked ways, then will I hear from heaven and will forgive their sin and heal their land."*

In our text, Joshua was calling the people to self examination and to put away all that was alien to the life of God and to absolute surrender of themselves to His service. Here then is our responsibility, for God's tomorrow waits for our day of Sanctification.

That is God's Eternal Law for blessings, for revival, for power, for miracles. Even in nature God has set unchanging laws and they never, like God's power, vary from day to day, if they were unreliable, how full of fear and uncertainty life would be. No man can disobey the law of gravity or electricity or steam without disaster. He knows the laws of that power must be obeyed or it will not only refuse to work for him but could actually destroy him.

To get into wrong relations with fire is to get burned, to get into wrong relations with electricity means instant death. The lesson is if we obey the law of the power, the power will work for us. While this is true of natural power, so it is with the spiritual. The Holy Spirit is constant in all His ways and workings. He acts according to the law of His power and if we obey those laws we can rely on Him but if we are neglectful He will withhold His power and blessing from us.

To blame the lack of revival and signs and wonders amongst us by saying, "God is Sovereign" is nothing short of libel on the love and mercy of God. This is but a cover for our shortcomings and failures. He was Sovereign when He wept over Jerusalem and He would have saved them but they would have none of it so it rendered Him unable to do anything. It is only when God's tide of power and blessing approaches mankind that it is stopped by a barrier of indifference and unbelief. Finney says,

> "There is one fact under government of God worthy of universal notice and everlasting remembrance. It is that, 'the most useful and important things are most easily and certainly obtained by the use of the appropriate means. This is evidently a principle in God's administration, and I fully believe that when the appointed means have been rightly used, spiritual blessings have been obtained with greater uniformity than temporal ones."

The appointed means are in our text, for tomorrow's display of power and miracles we need TODAY'S SANCTIFICATION. We need to set ourselves apart from the world to serve God with all our hearts.

SERMON 9

Believed

2 TIMOTHY 1:12

"I know whom I have believed"

Have you ever noticed how politicians, in opposition, deride every move of the government in power? Voices that were silent when they were in power now become the most raucous in denouncing those in office. How easy it is for the opposition who do not have to make a decision, whatever the outcome they are always right. If all goes well they say, "It could have been done better." If it goes wrong they say, "We told you so."

How easy it is to sit on the fence and criticise. Usually they are people with no firm convictions of their own. The Church is full of such, fence sitting, professing Christians who spend their time denouncing those who are in wholehearted service for Christ. While many of these professing Christians are writing books decrying the 'virgin birth,' the baptism of the Holy Spirit and the real power of Calvary's Cross. Paul the Apostle, still stands head and shoulders above them all and cries out, *"I know in whom I have believed."* (2 Timothy 1:12)

He had a personal experience of the Living God and did not depend on a once and for all Damascus Road experience. He had a daily knowledge of Christ. *"I die daily,"* (1 Corinthians 15:31) he said, *"And it is no longer I that liveth but Christ liveth in me."* (Galatians 2:20) He boldly declared HE whom he knew, before kings and princes, before judges and jailors and never once did his witness vary.

Why did Luther[1] and the Wesley's[2] have such a following? Simply because they knew in whom they had believed and declared it from the housetops. Why did Ian Paisley[3] have such a following in Ulster? Not because he was always right but because he had a fervent belief in what he was doing. Why does the Catholic Church still hold their own despite the enormous errors in it? Simply because she will not change her attitude or teachings for no man and you will be able to rely on them, however disastrously a hundred years hence.

While on the other hand the Protestants are changing almost weekly and it is no use saying because we are getting more understanding and more knowledge. The early Church spread like a prairie fire because they knew in whom they had believed and against all reason and common sense, they declared to the world that 'HE WAS ALIVE'. In Acts 2:32 Peter said, *"Jesus had God raised up, whereof we are all witnesses,"* an unlikely story but because of the certainty of their convictions they were believed and thousands were swept into the Kingdom of God.

I remember a young man in my church when he first started preaching he

---

[1] A German professor of theology who was a seminal figure in the Protestant Reformation. *https://en.wikipedia.org/wiki/Martin_Luther*
[2] John and Charles Wesley are among the most notable evangelists who ever lived. The Wesleyans and the Methodists are their offspring. Both preached and both wrote hymns. *https://christianhistoryinstitute.org/study/module/wesleys*
[3] Ian Richard Kyle Paisley, was a loyalist politician and Protestant religious leader from Northern Ireland. *https://en.wikipedia.org/wiki/Ian_Paisley*

would proclaim the truth and then say, "Well I think that's right anyway." I used to say to him, "It is not enough to think it's right, you must know for a certainty." Paul said, *"If the trumpet gives an uncertain sound who shall prepare himself for battle?"* (1 Corinthians 14:8) I ask you, Do you really know who you have believed? Do you know His will concerning salvation? Do you know His will concerning healing? Do you know His will concerning the baptism of the Holy Spirit?

Is it not because we don't know His will, we really don't know Him as we ought to, that so few are saved and healed and filled with the Holy Ghost? A great example of one who had lost the assurance was Thomas, the disciple of Jesus. He had no real certainty or real knowledge of Christ. The only way to win back his assurance was to go back to the source of his calling and abide there. *"Reach hither thy finger,"* said Jesus. The spirit of Thomas comes upon us all at some time or other but if we will but spare a moment in a quiet place we are sure to hear that same voice say, *"Reach hither thy finger."* (John 20:27)

How certain Paul was amidst all those philosophers on Mars Hill. He might, had he chosen, said many things to them, to which they might have listened with respect. He might have discussed morals, or he might have contrasted the ethical teaching of Christ with their own but this would have been for no purpose. The resurrection of Christ might provoke their mockery, the judgement to come, their anger but to have been silent about it would have given them a false idea of the gospel. It was more important that they should know the truth, whether they received it or not, than he should appease them with discussing things of no value. It may be however, that there are many things about God we do not understand and which cause us doubt, what then should we do? Christ Himself told us the way of certainty *"If any man will do to His will, he shall know of the doctrine whether it be of God."* (John 7:17)

The surrender of the will to God is always followed by an increase of spiritual knowledge and understanding. It is as true of the Sunday school teacher, as it is of the preacher that the Sabbath will be according to their weekly living. Let us all the week be absorbed in material things, let us seek only our own gratification, or wealth, or pleasure. Let us walk only in the paths of the ungodly, and then we need not be surprised if as we stand up on Sunday our voices have lost their old ring of joy and glory. We must not be astonished that our grasp of heavenly promises and provisions has slipped and that we speak in halting tones. If our daily walk is far from the Lord can we expect His presence and assurance on Sundays? Will not doubt then enter into our souls, will not uncertainty of His promises fail us and will not our faith weaken?

The certainty of Paul lays in the fact that he knew in whom he had believed for he had a daily walk with Him. We may feel frightened at times when scientists tell us about our mysterious relationship to animals and even to the lowest forms of vegetable life. However, there are many times in our life when we are conscious of a relationship of another kind and one that is linked to God above and that to us is of far greater importance and of greater reality than all their suppositions. We may know for sure where we have come from and we have a greater certainty of where we are going. We may not acknowledge our kinship to monkeys but we openly declare that we are in the family of God.

We may not know much about the laws of heat and light, or of the history of the world or even the structure of our own bodies but our hearts have been moved by a future that awaits us. We know about the authority of God, about the access we have to His presence, about judgement to come and above all, of a Father who is waiting to call us home. A home that He is preparing for us in the heaven of His glory. Scientists know nothing of this, they have nothing to thrill our souls with but they continue to pour forth their stories. We can say with the apostle John, *"We know we have eternal life, when we pray we know that He hears us and we know that we are of God and the whole world lieth in wickedness."* (1 John 5:19)

How much more should we who have the glorious certainties of the promises of God to stand on, boldly declare our faith to a lost world of sin. While science and the evolutionists have to say, "We must suppose;" we say "We know in whom we have believed and are persuaded that He is able to keep that which we have committed unto Him against that day." (see 2 Timothy 1:12)

SERMON 10

Glorified in His Saints

2 THESSALONIANS 1:10-12

"When he shall come to be glorified in his saints, and to be admired in all them that believe (because our testimony among you was believed) in that day. Wherefore also we pray always for you, that our God would count you worthy of this calling, and fulfil all the good pleasure of his goodness, and the work of faith with power: That the name of our Lord Jesus Christ may be glorified in you, and ye in him, according to the grace of our God and the Lord Jesus Christ."

God glorified in His saints is the simple yet compound evidence that God is. There are many testimonies that abound that prove the reality of the Living God, testimonies as witnessed by the sun, moon and stars. In fact they all declare the glory and reality of God. However, what God revealed in mankind is not only more positive evidence but it brings the presence and reality of God close to us and displays fully the character of God.

Just as through the life of Christ the fact of God was made plain and simple by the words He spoke, by the deeds He did and by how He responded to different situations He was confronted with. The fact that He was able to display the perfect character of God was because of His close relationship to Him. He dwelt, says John, in the bosom of His Father and He had been with Him from the beginning. (see John 1:18) So complete was the evidence of God in the life of Christ that He could without boasting declare, *"He that hath seen me hath seen the Father."* (John 14:9) Now a more complete and fuller revelation cannot be had than that.

Through Christ we have evidence that God is Love. Through Christ we have the evidence that God is Peace that He is joy and that He cares. For all these attributes were manifested in Christ. He is the perfect evidence that God is and that God is good.

Since Christ has passed this way and gone into glory, God now uses men as evidence that HE IS. It is what they see in us that determines their opinion of God. We all have met men, who by their tremendous sympathy and compassion, whose wisdom and counsel have been a shining influence on our lives, men through whom the very character of God is displayed.

When we meet these men we realise immediately what a tremendous testimony they are to the existence and to the character of Christ. They are no self originated personalities but lives that have been moulded to a pattern and that is the highest pattern. Seeing this, we can look up and say with them, *"He hath made us and not we ourselves."* (Psalm 100:3)

We see right through the Scriptures right through Christian history what effect men's lives have had in declaring who God is. When we look at such characters as Baalam our whole thought is concentrated on his braying ass. We have great difficulty in bringing to mind the wonderful soul enriching prophecies he made. The one ill-redeeming feature of his character, that of the love of money overshadows everything else in this remarkable man's life and all he reminds us of is his braying ass. How sad, what a poor reflection on God. The only evidence he leaves behind of God is that of an ass. Baalam was such a complex character, a man who could have done such great things for God but he left behind, simply the thoughts of the love of money.

We have again that notable character Jonah who by his disobedience leaves behind him not so much evidence of God but simply of a big fish, a whale. Oh! haven't the sceptics had a whale of a time with his evidence?

Thankfully, there are characters like the apostle John who throughout his writings, the very presence of God shines through. He doesn't have to prove God, he declares Him from the very first sentence of his gospel and then in each succeeding chapter goes on to display the wonderful character of God. How could he do this? Well, just like Him of whom he wrote he had leaned on His breast. He had been in close communion with Him from the beginning. Yes, even to the Isle of Patmos where he could declare, *"I was in the Spirit on the Lord's day."* (Revelations 1:10) Christ was able through him to make known to the world the dreadful awe inspiring scenes of the last days.

The saints and martyrs down through the ages have borne evidence and eloquent testimony of Christ. Their lives indicate what God is like. Their sufferings, on His behalf, were but a reflection of the sufferings He bore for them. Their joy and peace but a measure of the joy and peace that is His.

Might I be permitted to ask, what evidence is there in our lives that God exists, that HE IS? What evidence that He is good, caring, loving. As the old song says, "Is there enough evidence, if we were charged with being a Christian, to convict us?" Church membership is no proof, and church attendance is no evidence that God exists. Is there any likeness, any similarity in our behaviour to His? Is there any evidence that our behaviour comes from a higher source than ourselves? Do we overcome evil with good or do we return evil for evil? Can the world see a change in our behaviour? Has the hardness gone and a soft aura of love replaced it?

Do you ever go the extra mile? When someone pleads for your coat do you give them your cloak also? When you see someone destitute and broken do you bind up their wounds and clothe them and put them on your own ass? Do you tell the innkeeper to charge it to your account? If you see someone hungry do you feed them? If you see someone thirsty do you give them a drink? Jesus said, *"As much as you have done it unto the least of one of these, you have done it unto Me."* (Matthew 25:40)

In so doing, you have reflected by nature God's attitudes. These are but the basics of Christianity, the shallower waters. So, how shall we manage the deep waters if we are floundering in the shallows? How shall we manage the meat of the word if the milk causes us so much digestive problems?

A man was once caught impersonating a Peer of the Realm.[1] It was not his clothes that gave him away, nor even his talk, because he dressed and spoke exactly as the peer but he forgot to polish under his shoes. That to me was out of sight out of mind. Just a little detail but it trapped him. We might dress and talk like Christians but it is always one of the minor things of life that snares us and the evidence proves to all the world that we are not what we say we are. We are imposters and there is no God at

---

[1] A Peer of the Realm is a member of the highest aristocratic social order, outside the ruling dynasty of the kingdom.

all in us. God help us in the small things then the large things will take care of themselves.

Let us leave behind not only the fact that GOD IS, but by our lives, by our love, by our compassion, by our care for one another, that our God is a God of Love and HE cares for each individual so much that He gave His life for them that they might have abundant life.

A life with a hope of heaven at its end.

SERMON 11

No Balm in Gilead

JEREMIAH 8: 18-19

"When I would comfort myself against sorrow, my heart is faint in me. Behold the voice of the cry of the daughter of my people because of them that dwell in a far country: Is not the Lord in Zion? is not her king in her? Why have they provoked me to anger with their graven images, and with strange vanities?"

Here we find Jeremiah sick at heart and sorrowful. It seems he can find no respite for his grief; nothing can ease the pain he feels or stop the tears from falling. The reason for this great sorrow is the cry of his people up and down the length of the land. *"IS THE LORD NOT IN ZION - IS HER KING NOT HERE?"* (Jeremiah 8:19)

Why has the Lord forsaken us, why are we left destitute? When we call He will not hear, and our troubles are more than we can bear. Has He forever left us? Is not His presence in Zion anymore? He had always been there in the Temple for the Shekinah glory which was between the cherubim had constantly shone forth declaring His presence and His glory and while He was there the people were content.

So now that contentment had gone, the people were extremely anxious and they cried throughout the land, *"Is not the Lord in Zion, is not her King here?"* At this point God answers them, *"Why have you provoked me to anger with your graven images and with your foreign idols?"* (Jeremiah 8:19) They had left Him to worship the idols of the people around them. They had offered sacrifices to Baal and Rimmon, they had bowed the knee before them and the memory of the true God had been dismissed from their minds. Sadly, now they were in desperate trouble and neither Baal nor Rimmon could help them.

They had two seasons, the harvest for gathering the grain and the summer for gathering the fruit. If one failed they could always depend on the other but now they both have failed and they cried in their distress, *"The harvest is past, the summer is ended and we are not saved."* (Jeremiah 8:20) That of course is the literal translation but there is a spiritual application which portrays a people who have gone their own way ignoring God and the things of God, seeking the sensual pleasures of the people who knew not God and in their mad rush for personal pleasure the time has flown by, the harvest and summer had gone and they are left with nothing but despair.

They had watched others returning home as the sun dipped behind the hills, weary and worn with the toils of the day, gathering in their harvest. They pitied them and said there was plenty of time to do that later on. "Enjoy yourselves" they cried, but it was later than they thought, the harvest and summer had passed and their hands were empty. They cried in their distress but there was none to hear, none to soothe, none to comfort. Jeremiah looking upon the scene of distress in the God forsaken land cried out: *"Is there no balm in Gilead? Is there no physician there? Why then has the health of the daughters of my people not been restored?"* (Jerimiah 8:22)

The answer to the first question is, yes. Gilead was noted for its medical herbs and for its physicians. The answer to the third question is not that no remedy has been available but that the remedy had not been applied. We are living in a day and generation to which this is applicable. It is an undisputed fact that people have ignored God and counted as nothing the sufferings He bore on the cross on their behalf. They have disregarded the Spirit of Grace and today they are reaping their reward. Gloom and despondency is on every hand and there doesn't seem to be a way out.

People are searching for God today in greater numbers than ever before but it's not the Church of God that is leading them but every false cult and physician imaginable. Sadly, there is no comfort or solace in those and the cry rings out, *"IS THERE NO BALM IN GILEAD? IS THERE NO PHYSICIAN THERE?"* (Jerimiah 8:22)

Yes, there is balm in Gilead and the great physician Himself is there. *"Then why has the health of the daughters of my people not been restored?"* It is because there is no one to bring the medicine. At one point Jeremiah cried out: *"O that my head were waters and my eyes a fountain of tears that I might weep for the slain of the daughter of my people."* (Jeremiah 9:1)

Friends, out there are people yearning for the healing balm of our God and His dispensary is never empty. Yet we haven't sufficient care, sufficient pity and compassion to take it to them. We are withholding healing medicine from countless thousands. Let's offer our service to God today and let each one of us in response to His question, "WHO WILL GO?" Answer, "I will go Lord send me."

Out there are perils, the road is hard and the way is rough. You will find the 'Slough'[1] and 'Despond'[2]; you will find the 'Hill of Difficulty'[3] and the 'Valley of Humiliation'.[4] You will also reach the 'Golden Heights of Gladness'[5] from where you can see wonderful visions of' Beulah Land'.[6] However swiftly the scene changes for you, you may be sure that your provision in Christ is abundant. You will go into a big world and you will confront big things. There are obstacles to overcome, giants to slay, there is *"pestilence that walketh in darkness,"* the *"destruction that wasteth at noonday"*. (Psalm 91:6) There are the slain of the enemy everywhere, there is success, there is failure, there is sin and sorrow and death.

Pathetic plights on every hand, people sick, people dying and the cry going forth, *"Is there no balm in Gilead, is there no physician?"* Then we see the most pathetic sight of all, Mr Christian moving about this grim field professing to be a physician but carrying in his bag, no balm, no oil and no ointments to meet the terrific needs of the people.

That is the situation as it appears to me today and God graciously offered in abundance gifts through the Holy Spirit by whom pain can be alleviated, the suffering halted and the misery turned to joy. He has made provision but we have nothing in our bags and all I can say is "God help us". God be patient with us until we come to your storehouse and leave laden with good gifts for men; gifts of salvation, gifts of healing, gifts of peace and joy.

Then let us go out into the highways of life carrying all that is needed to the fainting, to the bruised, to those who are bound, to those who are sick, to those who are lonely and dispirited, with perfect confidence in

---

[1- 6] The Pilgrim's Progress from This World, to That Which Is to Come is a 1678 Christian allegory written by John Bunyan. It is regarded as one of the most significant works of religious, theological fiction in English literature. It has been translated into more than 200 languages, and has never been out of print. It has also been cited as the first novel written in English. *https://en.wikipedia.org/wiki/The_Pilgrim%27s_Progress*

Him in whom we have believed.

It's a wonderful calling, it's a glorious calling. The work is difficult but Him in whom you have confidence is mighty to save, to deliver, to set free, to heal and to comfort.

As you go forward you will find that the joy of the Lord will be your strength.

SERMON 12

Knowledge and Thought

JOB 17:11

"My days are past; my purposes are broken off, even the thoughts of my heart."

KNOWLEDGE is a wonderful thing but the pursuit of knowledge can engage our attention for years and years. It can mean many and as that wise man Solomon said, *"Much study is a weariness of the flesh."* (Ecclesiastes 12:12)

Now THOUGHT is so much greater than knowledge, in that, knowledge in anyone is extremely limited; but who can contain thought? It is available without limit from the youngest to the oldest.

Isn't it amazing that one of the greatest questions in Scripture demands the content of our thoughts? It doesn't ask us what we know of Christ but simply, "think ye of Christ?"

It is not what we know about Him that is important; it's what we think about Him. So now our thoughts motivate our spirit like the old gospel song says; "I think of Him He sways my soul with divine control whenever I think of Him."

But even thoughts have to be controlled and we are exhorted;

"Whatever things are true, whatsoever things are honest, whatsoever things are just, whatsoever things are pure, whatsoever things are lovely, whatsoever things are of good report, if there be any virtue and if there be any praise, think on these things." (Phillipians 4:8)

A man or woman whose thoughts dwell on these things is indeed a person who is dwelling in the secret places of the Most High; but there are two thoughts that are always uppermost in our minds. To the ambitious young people there is the thought of; visions of grandeur and glory. What can be? What can be accomplished? When we are old the thoughts that are pr-eminent are; what might have been? If only, If only what? Well, if only we had been a little more diligent in the faith, if we had only given more time to the work of the Lord. If only, if only, the list is endless.

There is another lesson we can learn from all this and that is, while thought is infinitely greater than knowledge, DOING is greater than thinking. There is a vast superiority of things really done to anything that is merely thought. People may have fine thoughts and purposes and even projects in their minds, they may have beautiful and magnificent things within them but if they are there only and go no further they are of little worth.

Things that exist merely in the mind however wonderful, what are they if they stop there and never come out? What purposes, what schemes, what projects have died a death in our thoughts? So, let something be done. Let something be achieved, let something be translated from mere thought into action. Oh! there is far more value in that. As the old blacksmiths song says; "Something attempted, something done, he has earned his nights repose."

There is far more value given in a cup of cold water given in His name than all our finest thoughts that never come to fruition. You may take the plan of an architect as it lies upon the paper. The drawing is very beautiful, the shading correct, it is all done properly to scale and as it lies before your eyes it really looks magnificent. Yet, you cannot live in it, it will not shelter you from the storm or the heat. Only, let that plan be worked out, let it cease to be simply a drawing but a solid structure, let it be the real thing, then you can walk in and out of it, you can have all the comfort of its conveniences and your body as well as your mind can enjoy it.,

Friends, there is all the difference between mere thinking and acting that there is between nonentity and reality. For we really do nothing as to the actual business while it is only a thought existing in our mind. After Paul exhorted those Philippians to think on those things which were eternal, he didn't finish there but went on to say; *"Those things which ye have both learned and received, and heard, and seen in me do, and the God of peace shall be with you."* (Philippians 4:9)

Still, how hard, how difficult, to translate thought into action. You may have the most wonderful and regal of thoughts but until they are brought into reality they are valueless. I am glad that the book which follows the four gospels is not called 'The Thoughts of the apostles' but the Acts of the apostles.

You may read the thoughts of chairman Mao, the old communist ruler of China but the Acts of the Apostles has stirred the world to follow the Lord. The Acts of the Apostles brought thousands into a saving knowledge of our Lord Jesus Christ. Their acts founded church after church throughout the world. Their acts demonstrated the power of God to heal, to quicken, to judge, to perform miracles. Their acts caused it to be said of them that they, "turned the world upside down." On the day of Pentecost their thoughts were changed into action, they became men of action.

Thinking requires no physical effort, no expense. You can sit down or even lie down and think. The gift of the Holy Spirit is given that we might transform our thoughts into action. It may well be that God hasn't called us to any wonderful work for Him that is in the public eye but that is no excuse for doing nothing.

God refused David permission to build the temple but he did not sit back and do nothing; no indeed rather he prepared an abundance of material for its building. He found nails, the gates, the joining, the brass, the gold and silver and timber and stone.

David had thought to build the house unto the name of the Lord his God. He had thought about it day and night. He had thought of its beauty and its glory and so it came as a shock when God said he could not build it. Although he was denied that joy, David prepared the materials for its buildings with all his heart and because of his labours that temple was erected.

He excited everyone with his zeal and his cry to the people was, *"Arise therefore and be doing, and the Lord be with thee."* (1 Chronicles 22:16) We may not be called to preach or teach but we can supply the materials necessary for a great harvest. Don't let us sit down and think what could happen, or what might happen? Let's turn our God given visions and thoughts into reality. Let us arise and be doing and I am sure that as He was with Moses so will He be with us. When Moses cried unto the Lord before the Red Sea, when the Egyptian army was almost upon them, God said, *"Wherefore thou criest unto Me. Speak to the children of Israel that they go."* (Exodus 14:15)

There is a time for prayer but if it is not followed by action then it is of no consequence. We have talked and thought and prayed for a mighty move of God, now let's bring it into reality by stepping out in faith, believing and putting Him to the test.

"Prove me now herewith, saith the Lord of hosts, if I will not open you the windows of heaven and pour you out a blessing that there shall not be room enough to receive it." (Malachi 3:10)

Printed in Great Britain
by Amazon